PSYCHOLOGY FOR PEACE ACTIVISTS:

A NEW PSYCHOLOGY

FOR THE GENERATION WHO CAN ABOLISH WAR

by

David Adams

The Advocate Press

New Haven, CT

Revised Edition

1995

*

reprinted 2015

2

TABLE OF CONTENTS

ACKNOWLEDGEMENTS

I am grateful to Irving Crain, George and Edie Fishman, Virginia Knowldon, Lindsay Mathews, Howard Parsons, Cecilia Pollack, Milton Schwebel, Bob Steele, and Alan Thomson for their encouragement and suggestions on the first edition. Figure credits belong to UNESCO/Dominique Rogier (photo, page 5), the Schomburg Center of the New York Public Library (cover photo, pages 15, 21, 45), Robert Sengstacke (page 21), Swarthmore College Peace Collection (pages 27 and 33), Tom Cornell, Ben Fernandez and the Marquette University Library (page 37), Tamiment Library of New York University (page 51), Helen Caldicott and WAND page 57), Cecilia Pollack (page 55) and Lindsay Mathews (page 78). The photo on page 63 was taken by the author.

Cover photo: Martin Luther King Jr. addressing the 1967 anti-Vietnam War rally in front of the United Nations.

PREFACE TO SECOND EDITION

In the decade since the first edition was conceived, peace activism has greatly broadened its focus.

In the earlier period, the world was stuck in the "quagmire of anti-communism", to quote the Reverend Martin Luther King. The world was held hostage by the Cold War and the nuclear arms race which threatened to destroy the world from one minute to another demanding the constant attention of peace activists.

With the end of the Cold War, peace activists have been able to refocus their attention more on the root causes of the war system. Working in thousands of non-governmental organizations (NGO's) around the world, they are addressing the political and economic injustices which, since the beginning of history, have led to war.

The United Nations and its specialized agencies have emerged from the paralysis of the Cold War and begun to accomplish the tasks for which they were designed fifty years ago "to save succeeding generations from the scourge of war."

As a result, the nation-state, long the monopolizer of organized violence and the bastion of the war system, has begun to yield power on both flanks - to the United Nations on a global level and to NGO's on a local level.

We can now see emerging the outlines of a global movement to replace the culture of war with a culture of peace. Disarmament remains essential to this movement, but it also links up with the struggles for democracy, human rights and for equitable, endogenous, sustainable development.

The first edition of this book focussed on the Cold War and on peace activists from one of the two super-powers involved, the U.S. Regrettably, an equal emphasis was not given to Soviet peace activists who, at that time, played an important role in ensuring that their country's dramatic transition took place without recourse to the terrible military force that was at their disposal.

Now that the attention of the peace movement has become truly global in scope, it is appropriate that this book should be expanded to include the perspective of a great peace activist from another part of the world: Nelson Mandela of South Africa.

The stages of consciousness development illustrated by Nelson Mandela in his autobiography, **Long Walk to Freedom,** are so similar to those described by American peace activists, that it makes a strong case for the universality of these processes - at least for the present moment of history. This is as it should be if we believe with Mandela and others that we are on the verge of a single global civilization and a global movement for a culture of peace.

As Mandela has put it, the changes in travel, communication and mass media have accelerated and now changes occur so fast it is difficult to keep up with them:

> "What struck me so forcefully was how small the planet had become during my decades in prison; it was amazing to me that a teenage Innuit living at the roof of the world could watch the release of a political prisoner on the Southern tip of Africa. Television had shrunk the world; and had in the process become a great weapon for eradicating ignorance and promoting democracy."

Like other activists described in first edition of this book, Nelson Mandela is very explicit about the importance for him of the basic values of freedom, integrity and democracy received from his extended family, the tribe and culture. Throughout the most difficult years of his imprisonment, he shared a sense of purpose with his colleagues and resisted the attempts of the prison authorities "to exploit every weakness, demolish every initiative, negate all signs of individuality - all with the idea of stamping out that spark that makes each of us human and each of us who we are."

In a few pages of lucid prose, he explains how he came to be an activist:

> I had no epiphany, no singular revelation, no moment of truth, but a steady accumulation of a thousand slights, a thousand indignities and a thousand unremembered moments produced in me an anger, a rebelliousness, a desire to fight the system that imprisoned my people. There was no particular day on which I said, Henceforth I will devote myself to the liberation of my people; instead, I simply found myself doing so, and could not do otherwise.

Even in prison he and his colleagues maintained their activism: "we regarded the struggle in prison as a microcosm of the struggle as a whole. We would fights inside as we had fought outside. As a result, "there were many dark moments when my faith in humanity was sorely tested, but I would not and could not give myself up to despair."

Mandela illustrates throughout his book the skills of affiliation. Although he often found himself on the losing side of policy debates, he would always swallow his pride and respect the collective decision. At times he learned from his errors and changed his opinion; at other times it was his views that eventually convinced the others and prevailed. It was always a process of patience, of listening, and of growth:

> I have always believed that to be a freedom fighter one must suppress many of the personal feelings that make one feel like a separate individual rather than part of a mass movement. One is fighting for the liberation of millions of people, not the glory of one individual.

At the same time, however, there were moments when he had to make decisions alone - such as his decision to initiate discussion with the apartheid regime:

> I knew that my colleagues upstairs would condemn my proposal, and that would kill the initiative even before it was born. There are times when a leader must move out ahead of the flock, go off in a new direction, confident that he is leading his people the right way.

Mandela describes the importance, the difficulties, the successes and failures of personal integration. Through two marriages and a law practice which was eventually destroyed, he remained in touch with his need for family:

> When your life is the struggle, as mine was, there is little room left for family. That has always been my greatest regret, and the most painful aspect of the choice I made.

Finally, we can learn much of leadership and world historic consciousness from his example. He was never sectarian. Despite differences with tribal leaders, despite challenges from a new generation, despite outright sabotage from the PAC and Chief Buthelezi, he always maintained a dialogue with them, seeking to convince them of the values of unity and learning whatever he could from their experiences and perspectives.

Mandela and his colleagues have added greatly to our understanding of non-violence through their constant struggle over the issue:

> I saw non-violence on the Gandhian model not as an inviolable principle but as a factor to be used as the situation demanded. The principle was not so important that the strategy should be used even when it was self-defeating, as Gandhi himself believed. I called for non-violent protest for as long as it was effective.

In what is perhaps his greatest contribution, he sought out and maintained dialogue with the oppressors. In the spirit of Gandhi, he knew "that the oppressor must be liberated just as surely as the oppressed." In explaining how he could accept the Nobel Peace Prize jointly with South African President de Klerk, he says, "To make peace with an enemy, one must work with that enemy, and that enemy becomes your partner."

His leadership was always based on respect and close touch with the people, even during the long years in prison. "To lead one's people, one must truly know them." In his early days during the defiance campaign, he toured the country, sometime going from one house to another in the townships: "we had to win people over one by one." From the beginning he saw it was foolhardy to go against the people: "It is no use to take an action to which the masses are opposed, for it will then be impossible to enforce."

He describes his role as a "promoter of unity, an honest broker, a peacemaker" and his mission as one "of preaching reconciliation, of binding the wounds of the country, of engendering trust and confidence."

Mandela emerged from his experiences with a consciousness that is truly global in scope:

> I was first and foremost an African nationalist fighting for our emancipation from minority rule and the right to control our own destiny. But, at the same time South Africa and the African continent were part of the larger world. Our problems, while distinctive and special, were not unique, and a philosophy that placed these problems in an international and historical context of the greater world and the course of history was valuable

Challenged to dissociate himself from the communists who had a similar global view, he refused to do so, despite pressure from the government, the international community, rival organizations like the PAC, and many in the ranks of his own ANC. Although he had begun his activism as an anti-

Awarding of the Houphouet-Boigny Prize for Peace by Federico Mayor to Nelson Mandela and Frederick DeKlerk at UNESCO, 3 February 1992
photo credit: UNESCO/Dominque Rogier

communist and even broken up communist meetings in his early years, his autobiography richly illustrates how he came to value the contribution that communists make to the struggle and the strength that comes from an alliance with them.

The reader is invited to compare this picture of the steps of consciousness development of Nelson Mandela with those of the other great peace activists described in the earlier edition of this book. I believe that the reader will find them so similar that it gives support to the possibility of a global consciousness for a culture of peace which can develop in cultures through the world.

At the present moment of history it is possible that an additional step is being added to those of consciousness development: a step of vision. Mandela exemplifies a new generation of peace activists whose actions provide a vision for a peaceful world. Not content to struggle against the vicious, anti-human system of apartheid, Mandela and his fellow activists in the ANC had the courage and foresight to develop the Freedom Charter which provides not only a vision for South Africa, but by extension for the rest of the world as well. [1].

As Mandela describes, the Freedom Charter was developed by a process that evoked suggestions from ordinary people throughout the country. The responded to a call asking them "How would you set about making South Africa a happy place for all the people who live in it?" The Freedom Charter "captured the hopes and dreams of the people, and acted as a blueprint for the liberation struggle and the future of the nation."

The vision in the Freedom Charter is remarkably similar to that of the Universal Declaration of Human Rights which was formulated in those years by the United Nations. It is at once specific and universal, practical and visionary.

The vision of the Freedom Charter was further elaborated later by the ANC in preparation for the first free elections in South Africa. As Mandela says, "Some in the ANC wanted to make the campaign simply a liberation election and tell the people vote for us because we set you free. We decided instead to offer them a vision of the South Africa we hoped to create."

Today, to paraphrase Mandela, peace activists can do more than just be against the war system, but they can at the same time act to bring a universal vision closer to reality. In opposing the culture of war, today's activist can help construct a culture of peace.

PSYCHOLOGY FOR PEACE ACTIVISTS:
A NEW PSYCHOLOGY FOR THE GENERATION WHO CAN
ABOLISH WAR

Each new stage of history demands a new psychology - one that can explain and support the psychological development of the people who must undertake the most important tasks on the historical agenda.

In our time, a new task has risen to the top of the historical agenda - the abolition of war and the replacement of its culture by a culture of peace. This has occurred as a result of great historical changes as foreseen in the famous 1932 correspondence between Albert Einstein and Sigmund Freud, in which Freud wrote:

> These two factors - man's cultural disposition and a well-founded fear of the form that future wars will take - may serve to put an end to war...But by what ways or byways this will come about we cannot guess.

Although the process is still not clear, we may be sure that it will involve the mobilization of people at every level, of peace movements composed of individual peace activist, for whom the question of their consciousness is crucial.

History demands a new psychology. But history does not act in the abstract. Since peace will be achieved by movements composed of individual peace activists, it is for you, the peace activist, that the new psychology is needed, and it is to you that this book is dedicated.

To begin the development of the new psychology, I have sought in the first section to gain lessons from the lives of our fore-runners, the great U.S. peace activists of the 20th Century. In their autobiographies we find the steps of their consciousness development and the psychological difficulties that they faced at each step. Six steps - and corresponding sets of difficulties - may be distinguished, and we will consider each one of them in turn: values and purpose vs. alienation; anger vs. fear and pessimism; action vs. armchair theorizing; affiliation vs. anarchism; integration vs. burnout; and world-historic consciousness vs. sectarianism.

To foresee the questions that will be asked of the new psychology, in the second section I have sought its root causes in the economic and political changes that have brought peace to the top of the historical agenda.

The concluding section of the book outlines the tasks of the new psychology. The new psychology can develop only through the efforts of many people including activists, psychologists and, most especially, psychologists who are activists. Therefore the final section of this book is addressed not only to peace activists, but also to professional psychologists and young people who will become the psychologists of the future. All of us must work together to create the new psychology and carry out its great historical tasks.

LESSONS FROM THE LIVES OF GREAT PEACE ACTIVISTS:
SIX STEPS OF CONSCIOUSNESS DEVELOPMENT

The new psychology is foreshadowed in the lives of the great peace activists who have gone before us. We can learn from them as they traveled the road that we must take in the struggle to abolish war.

I have taken a case history approach and chosen the lives of ten great peace activists to analyze. For the most part I have been inductive and let their autobiographies speak for themselves about important psychological issues. But, like any psychologist, I bring certain tools and theoretical approaches to the work. In previous studies, I have developed this approach through studies of other autobiographies, oral histories of local peace activists, statistical analysis of why students become peace activists, studies of the physiology and psychology of motivational systems, and study of the general principles of activity psychology as it was developed in the Soviet Union [2]. Also, I am a peace activist myself, and have studied the history of American peace movements [3].

In deciding which ten peace activists to choose, I have concentrated on Americans and sought a broad range of activists who rose to leadership from the various peace constituencies. Because my audience is primarily the U.S. peace movement, I have chosen our fore-runners in particular. They represent the broad range of the U.S. peace movement. There are five women and five men. Four were Nobel Prize winners, three of whom won the Nobel Prize for Peace. There is the remarkable Eugene Victor Debs, who received almost a million votes for President while confined to prison for opposing World War I. There are heroes of the movement to end the war in Vietnam in which many activists of my generation first got involved. And I have included two activists who helped organize today's mass peace movement in the United States, Helen Caldicott and Sandy Pollack. A special note is needed for Sandy who died at the age of 36 in a plane crash and who, as the eulogies in her book testify, was better known abroad than in the United States. She symbolizes a new and increasingly important aspect of the U.S. peace movement that may be said to have begun with Jane Addams, an internationalism that seeks to unify the peace and justice movements of the entire world.

In considering the consciousness development of these

great activists, it is not possible to separate the goal of peace from the goal of social justice.   Jane Addams and Emily Balch won Nobel Peace Prizes for their work for peace, but each was involved in the movement for women's rights as well, and each began her consciousness development in social work on behalf of exploited people, including immigrant workers who came to America before the turn of the Century. Dorothy Day and Bertrand Russell are best known as peace activists, but both began their activism on behalf of women's suffrage. Day was imprisoned for participating in a suffrage march in 1917, and Russell ran for British Parliament in 1907 on a women's suffrage platform.   Day later founded the Catholic Worker Movement, and Russell, having become a world famous mathematician, philosopher, and writer, helped mobilize scientists' opposition to nuclear armament and later the CND and Committee of 100 for nuclear disarmament in England.

Both W.E.B. DuBois and Martin Luther King, Jr. came to the peace movement by way of their struggles for civil rights. DuBois founded the NAACP in the first decade of the 20th Century and edited its publication **The Crisis** for many decades.   And the journey of Martin Luther King Jr. from civil rights to trade union struggles to opposition to the Vietnam War and the Nobel Peace Prize is a well-known story.

Both Eugene Victor Debs and A.J. Muste came out of

the labor movement. Debs was the principal organizer of the great national railroad strike of 1894 and only later became a socialist, a Presidential candidate, and an anti-war activist. A.J. Muste, having resigned his pulpit over pacifist opposition to World War I, was thrust by chance into the leadership of a bitter textile strike in Lawrence, Massachusetts, where his consciousness rapidly developed. Later he played a major role in the civil rights movement and anti-Vietnam War movement. More recently Helen Caldicott and Sandy Pollack played leadership roles in the great anti-war movement of the 1980's. Caldicott first became active against the environmental effects of nuclear testing, and later worked with Australian trade unionists and American physicians against nuclear war.   And Sandy Pollack, in addition to her work against the Vietnam War and the escalation of the Cold War in the 1980's, began her political work as a leader of an   SDS housing committee in Boston which organized a tenants' council, rent strikes, and housing demonstrations.   Later she became a leader of solidarity work with the revolutionary movements of Latin America.

Consciousness development is something that we all know about from our own experience, whether or not we are peace activists.   To some extent, we all develop through similar steps, starting with the basic values and purpose that we learn from our family and friends and school. We become active, changing the world around us, and we affiliate with various organized groups, and develop a unique, integrated pattern of social relationships that we call personality and that is unlike that of anyone else. In this way, we become conscious of our self in relation to the rest of the world and to human history. The steps of this development may take place over a long period of time, as long as a lifetime, or sometimes they may occur very rapidly. Like the steps in a staircase - and unlike the stepping stones across a stream - each new step builds upon the preceding steps and interacts with them in a cumulative way. No development is lost, but each new step strengthens and transforms the steps that have gone before into a new and higher level of functioning.

In the autobiographies of the great peace activists, we find a pattern of consciousness development that can be described as six cumulative steps. They are: 1) acquisition of values and purpose; 2) anger; 3) action; 4) affiliation; 5) personal integration; and 6) world-historic consciousness. The steps tend to be taken in the order mentioned, although we should not forget that they are cumulative so that each step continues to operate in combination with later steps at a higher level of functioning [4]. We will find it useful to consider each step in terms of its opposite, i.e., the difficulties that can hinder development at that step: 1) alienation; 2) fear and pessimism; 3) armchair theorizing; 4) individualism and anarchism; 5) burnout; and 6) sectarianism.

ACQUISITION OF VALUES AND PURPOSE VS. ALIENATION

The consciousness development of the great peace activists begins, as in all of us, as a reflection of the values of society. These are learned by imitation and through formal instruction. In the process, we come to see the purpose of our lives in terms of what we can contribute to society and to human history. It can be said that such consciousness is what links the physiological and psychological processes of our individual lives to the political and economic processes of history.

The acquisition of values and purposes is not a passive process, but it is an active process in which the growing person reaches out, grasps, and integrates social values and molds them into a personal sense of destiny and purpose. In writing about her husband, Coretta Scott King describes the process like the unfolding drama of a play:

> Though I had been opposed to going to Montgomery,
> I realize now that it was an inevitable part of a

greater plan for our lives. Even in 1954 I felt that my husband was being prepared - and I too - for a special role about which we would learn more later. Each experience that we had was preparation for the next one. Being in Montgomery was like a drama that was unfolding. Martin and I and the people of that small southern city were like actors in a play,the end of which we had not yet read. Yet we felt a sense of destiny, of being propelled in a certain positive direction.

The acquisition of values and purpose is a social process. It occurs within a social context, beginning usually in the family. The values that Martin Luther King Jr. integrated into his life purpose came literally from his mother's lap. King wrote how his mother told him about slavery, the Civil War, and the establishment of segregation, and "she said the words that almost every Negro hears before he can understand the injustice that makes them necessary: 'You are as good as anyone.'" The family of Sandy Pollack was politically involved and her parents "tried to bring some political consciousness into her life" by starting a social action club for teenagers where "kids discussed issues presented by speakers once a month...and held folk-song 'hootenannies.'" And the initiation of Eugene Debs into the Brotherhood of Locomotive Firemen was the fulfillment of his father's passionate commitment to the ideals of the French Revolution: Liberty, Equality, Fraternity. From then on, it was "the spirit of the working class" that gave him commitment:

> I rode on the engines over mountain and plain, slept in the cabooses and bunks, and was fed from their pails by the swarthy stokers who still nestle close to my heart, and will until it is cold and still. Through all these years I was nourished at Fountain Proletaire. I drank deeply of its waters and every particle of my tissue became saturated with the spirit of the working class.

The question of family purpose may recur later in life such as the renewed commitment that occurs at the birth of a child. For example, Dorothy Day began to emerge from her "long loneliness" of alienation when her daughter Tamar was born. Putting her quest for purpose in religious terms, she wrote, "there had been the physical struggle, the mortal combat almost, of giving birth to a child, and now there was coming the struggle for my own soul." Helen Caldicott says that with the birth of her first child, she realized "that I would die to save the lives of my children. At that moment I accepted personal responsibility for stopping the nuclear arms race."

Religion often extends and expresses the family values and purpose. For A. J. Muste, the church "was the center of social life and culture, as well as of worship and religious training" for his family as he was growing up. And later, as an ordained minister, facing the crisis of World War I, Muste found that "it was a problem which I could not evade because I had been brought up to take religion, specifically the Biblical teaching and Gospel ethic, seriously....the demand that is placed upon us because we belong to the family of man - that we be honest and pure and that we love all men." Similarly, Emily Green Balch, aged 10, responded to a "challenge" from her minister to "enlist....in the service of goodness" and years later she recalled, "I think I never abandoned in any degree my desire to live up to it."

The love of the family gives values an emotional warmth and power. All other values, in the church and in commitment to social justice, are based upon the love of the family, and it is against this love that all human relations are measured and by which they are judged. In the words quoted above from Muste, we must fight for peace and justice because we all "belong to the family of man." And in the words of Martin Luther King Jr.:

> At the center of nonviolence stands the principle of love....When we speak of loving those who oppose us....we speak of a love which is....understanding, redeeming good will for all men....a recognition of the fact that all life is interrelated. All humanity is involved in a single process, and all men are brothers.

The question of purpose arises especially when young people leave home such as when they go away to school.

Encouraged by the "broadening" influence of higher education students may inspire each other to reach out and take up a social purpose. W.E.B. DuBois, one of the generation of Black students who gained their education after the emancipation of the slaves, shared in a vision of his fellow graduates in a "program for freedom and progress among Negroes." "I replaced my hitherto egocentric world by a world centering and whirling about my race in America." Jane Addams, as one of the generation of women who went to college for the first time, shared in the enthusiasm of her fellow graduates for their "precious ideals....way of martyrdom and high purpose we had marked out for ourselves." The sense of purpose gained by Bertrand Russell at the university was more individualist, but no less demanding and idealistic: "I walked by myself in the Tiergarten and made projects of future work....one series of books on the philosophy of the sciences....and another series of books on social questions." It was a life's work that he never abandoned. Reading and studying makes it possible to reach out beyond the confines of family, church, and school and to adopt values from the whole range of human ex- perience. For Dorothy Day it was the way to find her purpose in life. Already, at the age of 15, she was an avid reader of

W.E.B. DuBois, founder of the NAACP and opponent of imperialism: "In college I replaced my hitherto egocentric world by a world centering and whirling about my race."
photo credit: Schomburg Center of the New York Public Library

Carl Sandburg, Jack London, and Upton Sinclair:

> though my only experience of the destitute was in
> books....[they] made me feel that from then on my life
> was to be linked to theirs, their interests were to be
> mine: I had received a call, a vocation, a direction to
> my life."

In autobiography after autobiography, one is struck by the
passion with which the great peace activists read and studied
in an active search for the acquisition of values, truth, and
purpose.

The activists of today become the role models for the activists of tomorrow. Thus, the life of Eugene Victor Debs was an inspiration to A.J. Muste and Dorothy Day. Jane Addams was an inspiration to Emily Greene Balch. Bertrand Russell was an inspiration to Balch and to Helen Caldicott. W.E.B. DuBois was an inspiration to Martin Luther King, Jr. Even if this book does nothing else, it should help supply role models to tomorrow's generation of activists. Not everyone has the opportunity to develop a life's purpose when growing u p - and instead may simply "go to work for the company." The following description by a peace activist, recalling his life before getting involved in the movement, sounds like the classic description of the alienation of the wage worker:

> I lived in a small town where there was never much comment on social concerns....I got married right away and we proceeded to have a family and that's almost totally consuming. I worked for a railroad company for a while and just let the world go by. That went on 12 years or so until the railroad went bankrupt....Otherwise I probably would have stayed there the rest of my life.

It is not only the worker who may lose a sense of purpose and become alienated. After Jane Addams graduated from college, she felt "disconnected" and "disillusioned" and she describes how she reached the lowest depths "of my nervous depression and sense of maladjustment." She later wrote perceptively about the alienation of young people with higher education who "feel a fatal want of harmony between their theory and their lives, a lack of coordination between thought and action." She described how some may become perpetual students and be "buried beneath this mental accumulation with lowered vitality and discontent." Her story is echoed repeatedly in the autobiographies of Bertrand Russell and Dorothy Day, including the title of the latter's autobiography, **The Long Loneliness**. Addams suggested involvement in the Settlement House movement as an answer to alienation, but she could equally have suggested involvement in the peace movement for a later generation.

Just as purpose is acquired in a social context, so, too, it may be lost and alienation may set in when a person becomes socially isolated. Having left the U.S. (and his Negro friends) to travel to Europe, DuBois noted in his diary, "I wonder what I am - I wonder what the world is - I wonder if life is worth the Sturm." Jailed and isolated for her part in a demonstration for women's suffrage, Dorothy Day recalls how "I lost all consciousness of any cause. I had no sense of being radical, making protest against a government, carrying on a nonviolent revolution. I could only feel darkness and desolation....I lost all feeling of my own identity....what was good and evil." Even

Martin Luther King Jr. was deeply affected by prison and solitary confinement: "Those hours were the longest and most frustrating and bewildering of my life."

Reaffirmation of the social context may renew the sense of purpose and dispel the despair of alienation. When King was released from jail, he was restored to faith in the struggle by the greeting he received:

> As I walked out the front door and noticed the host of friends and well-wishers, I regained the courage that I had temporarily lost. I knew that I did not stand alone....From that night on my commitment to the struggle for freedom was stronger than ever before.

The acquisition of values and purpose is only a beginning of consciousness development. Further development depends not only upon ideas, but must come through practice as well, which is what the rest of this book will consider. But practice for justice and peace, in a society dominated by militarism and material gain does not come easily. It takes courage and motivation, the key to which is the emotion of anger.

ANGER VS. FEAR AND PESSIMISM

In one autobiography after another we find the same story - the initial action for peace and justice is motivated by anger against injustice. Like the spark that ignites the fuel in an engine, anger is the stimulus that initiates action [5].

It was anger that transformed W.E.B. DuBois from a scholar, brilliant but ineffective in a world of exploitation and racism, into a powerful activist for civil rights:

> At the very time when my studies were most successful, there cut across this plan which I had as a scientist, a red ray which could not be ignored. I remember when it first, as it were, startled me to my feet....The news met me: Sam Hose had been lynched, and they said that his knuckles were on exhibition at a grocery store....I began to turn aside from my work....One could not be a calm, cool, and detached scientist while Negroes were lynched, murdered, and starved.

A bit later in his autobiography, DuBois describes how anger eventually stimulated him into activity, the founding of the Niagara Movement which later developed into the NAACP:

> But when Trotter went to jail, my indignation over-flowed. I did not always agree with Trotter then or later. But he was an honest, brilliant, unselfish man, and to treat as a crime that which was at worst mistaken judgment was an outrage. I sent out from Atlanta in June 1905 a call to a few selected persons

"for organized determination and aggressive action...."

In recalling his activities on behalf of conscientious objectors in World War I, which began his long career of peace activism, Bertrand Russell explains how he had become "filled with despairing tenderness towards the young men who were to be slaughtered, and with rage against all the statesmen of Europe." Similarly, Helen Caldicott, inspired a generation later by the example of Bertrand Russell, took her first steps of peace action when "I became indignant."

Not all anger is useful for consciousness development. The anger that can be harnessed to action and consciousness development is anger directed against the institutions of war and injustice, rather than anger directed against individuals as such. "You must not harbor anger," Martin Luther King Jr. admonished himself at one point in his autobiography when speaking about a personal anger. But in describing the growing demand for bus desegregation in Montgomery, King made it clear that anger is essential as a motive for action, as "there had developed beneath the surface a slow fire of discontent, fed by the continuing indignities and inequities to which the Negroes were subjected." Debs, upon his release from prison in 1895 where he had been confined in order to break the national railway strike, expressed it this way: "there has been no liberty in the world....for the maintenance of which man has not been required to fight." He was echoing the motto of Frederick Douglass, the American slave who fought his way to freedom and became a hero of the emancipation a generation before: "without struggle, there can be no progress."

Martin Luther King Jr., Nobel Peace Laureate: "the supreme task is to organize and unit people so that their anger becomes a transforming force"
Photo Credit: Robert Sengstacke and Shomburg Center of NY Public Library

If anger is not guided by the optimism of vision and clear humanistic values, it can be diverted into desperate and anti-human activities. The enemies of peace and justice often try to exploit anger in order to divert movements into such desperation [6].   We later learned that the FBI itself was involved in trying to provoke and divert the leadership of Martin Luther King, Jr., although we may never know who gave the order to bomb his home in 1956. The bombing threatened to turn the nonviolent movement for bus desegregation that he was leading into a "race riot" which could have become the "darkest night in Montgomery's history":

> I was immediately driven home. As we neared the scene I noticed hundreds of people with angry faces in front of the house....One Negro was saying to a policeman, who was attempting to push him aside: "I ain't gonna move nowhere. That's the trouble now; you white folks is always pushin' us around. Now you got your .38 and I got mine; so let's battle it out." As I walked toward the front porch, I realized that many people were armed.   Nonviolent resistance was on the verge of being transformed into violence.

King calmed the crowd and harnessed their anger to the work of the movement, calling for Christian values and optimism:

> Jesus still cries out in words that echo across the centuries: "Love your enemies; bless them that curse

you; pray for them that despitefully use you." This is what we must live by. We must meet hate with love. Remember, if I am stopped, this movement will not stop, because God is with the movement. Go home with this glowing faith and this radiant assurance.

Anger is not the same as violence. While President Reagan has ordered many violent actions, including the most dangerous military buildup in world history, he is said to be almost devoid of emotions by those who have seen him in private visits. After visiting Reagan, Helen Caldicott described him as a man without empathy, "like a cardboard photograph." In contrast, Gandhi, the greatest teacher of nonviolence, explains in his autobiography how he learned to reserve his anger from minor encounters and harness it later "for fighting bigger battles." In adopting Gandhi's nonviolent methods to the U.S. struggle for civil rights, Martin Luther King, Jr. explained:

> Nonviolent resistance is not a method for cowards; it does resist. If one uses this method because he is afraid or merely because he lacks the instruments of violence, he is not truly nonviolent. This is why Gandhi often said that if cowardice is the only alternative to violence, it is better to fight.... while the nonviolent resister is passive in the sense that he is not physically aggressive toward his opponent, his mind and emotions are always active, constantly seeking to persuade his opponent that he is wrong. The method is passive physically, but strongly active spiritually. It is not passive non-resistance to evil, it

is active nonviolent resistance to evil.

In the dynamic mechanisms of the human brain, anger and fear are opposing forces. [7]. This fact was recognized by Martin Luther King, Jr., who pointed out that fear can suppress anger, while anger can produce the courage that overcomes fear:

> The long repressed feelings of resentment on the part of the Negroes had begun to stir. The fear and apathy which had for so long cast a shadow on the life of the Negro community were gradually fading before a new spirit of courage and self-respect.

It is on the battleground of the mind, with the weapons of fear and anger that many of the most important struggles take place between the forces of peace and the forces of militarism. On the political level, fear of the "enemy" is constantly evoked by government statements and is echoed by the mass media in order to justify the arms race. On the psychological level, fear is used to intimidate leaders and discourage people from affiliating with movements for social change. We have seen how the tactics of fear were used in the bombing of King's home in Montgomery. But that was only part of a coordinated campaign that was almost successful:

> Almost immediately after the protest started we had begun to receive threatening telephone calls and

>letters. Sporadic in the beginning, they increased as
>time went on. By the middle of January, they had
>risen to thirty and forty a day....as the weeks passed,
>I began to see that many of the threats were in
>earnest. Soon, I felt myself faltering and growing in
>fear. One day, a white friend told me that he had
>heard from reliable sources that plans were being
>made to take my life.

Of course, in 1968, such a threat was carried out and King was assassinated. But during the intervening 13 years, King had overcome the fear, turned resentment into courage, and led a nation towards justice and peace.

Anger and fear are often mixed together. Jane Addams traced her early involvement in the movement for social justice to a vision of the poor in London that filled her with "despair and resentment." Emily Balch had a similar response to "a man fumbling with his bare fingers in an ash barrel to try to find something to eat." For years she had seen misery and starvation and "sickening" experiences "so bad that she hated to appear to acquiesce" in the system of capitalism, but this vision was "somehow final, and led her to call herself a Socialist." And Dorothy Day responded to her imprisonment after the demonstration for women's suffrage with such a mixture of fear and anger that she was totally exhausted by the experience.

There has been so much social pressure against the

expression of anger in our culture that it is often unrecognized or repressed [8]. And if anger is repressed, then fear may be left as the dominant emotion. Psychologists often find that their patients are unable to say that they are angry at injustice, but will label their emotion as "anxiety" instead. Such repression of anger can lead to helplessness. Dorothy Day became inactive for many years after her jail experience, and although she does not describe the process in herself, she describes it vividly in her husband Forster:

> He personally had not been in jail, but his rage at the system which confined political agitators to jail ate into him. And yet he did nothing but enclose himself into a shell, escape out on the bay with his fishing, find comfort in digging for clams or bait, or seek refuge in tending a garden.

If fear wins out, the anger may be turned inward and lead to self-destructive behavior. When A.J. Muste was angered by the hypocrisy of patriotic support for World War I, he found himself "at the point where I must feel myself doing something that costs and hurts, something for humanity, and God, or go stark mad." Fortunately for us, Muste did not turn the anger inward, but became involved in union organizing where he expressed his anger by joining with workers who were on strike.

If fear wins out against anger, a person's thinking can come to be dominated by pessimism. Of course, some pessimism comes from practical experience. As Helen Caldicott puts it, "the international balance of terror, economic pressures, and the frustration of dealing with a biased government and unresponsive bureaucracy leave many Americans feeling helpless." But pessimism also takes the form of irrational ideas and myths, such as the myth that human nature is intrinsically evil and war-like [9]. Alienated from working people because of their support for World War I, Bertrand Russell fell victim to the myth of the instinct of war and adopted a pessimistic view of humanity reduced "to primitive barbarism, letting loose, in a moment, the instincts of hatred and blood lust against which the whole fabric of society has been raised." Crippled by what he called "utter cynicism," Russell was unable to move forward to the next step of consciousness because "I was having the greatest difficulty in believing that anything at all was worth doing."

At higher levels of consciousness development, anger, unlike fear, can be harnessed by affiliation and put to work as a powerful force for social change. Rather than the emotion of a single individual setting forth into action, it becomes the battle cry of the movement. Martin Luther King saw this as a critical truth and a secret of the success of W.E.B. DuBois as a leader of the civil rights and peace movements: "History had taught him it is not enough for people to be angry - the supreme task is to organize and unite people so that their anger becomes a transforming force."

ACTION VS. ARMCHAIR THEORIZING

Action is the central step of consciousness development. In the peace movement, it distinguishes the peace activist. In psychology, it distinguishes the new psychology as a psychology of action. All other aspects of consciousness development may be distinguished in terms of whether they come before or after the initial action: some are precursors; other are consequences that come later as a result of action. As we have already seen, the step of values and purposes and the step of anger are precursors that lay the base and motivate action (although these steps continue to develop and intensify along with the other steps that come later).

On the question of peace, there are many people who never develop to the point of action. We have all met people who seem to share our values, purpose and anger for peace and justice, but who, for one reason or another, preach only "armchair theory" and "dry-as-dust gospel," as described by Martin Luther King Jr.:

> A faithful few had always shown a deep concern for social problems, but too many had remained aloof from the area of social responsibility. Much of this indifference, it is true, stemmed from a sincere feeling that ministers were not supposed to get mixed up in such earthly temporal matters as social and economic improvements; they were to "preach the gospel," and keep men's minds centered on "the heavenly." But however sincere, this view of religion, I felt, was too confined....Any religion that professes to be concerned with the souls of men and is not concerned with the slums that damn them, the economic conditions that strangle them, and the social conditions that cripple them is a dry-as-dust religion.

King could easily have been speaking about certain university professors in the same words he used for religious ministers.

The first step into action may be quite dramatic for those who come from professions in the church or universities where armchair theorizing predominates. For example, the initial action of Jane Addams that launched her entire career of social work began when she was wandering "disconnected" and "disillusioned" in Europe following her vision of "despair and resentment" in London:

> It is hard to tell just when the very simple plan which afterward developed into the Settlement began to form itself in my mind. It may have been even before I went to Europe for the second time, but I gradually became convinced that it would be a good thing to rent a house in a part of the city where many primitive and actual needs are found, in which young women who had been given over too exclusively to study, might restore a balance of activity along traditional lines and learn of life from life itself.

Similarly, the crucial decision of Martin and Coretta King to move from Boston to Montgomery, Alabama, was made because "in spite of the disadvantages and inevitable sacrifices, our greatest service could be rendered in our native South....We never wanted to be considered detached spectators." As they anticipated, this move placed them right in the middle of the unfolding drama of the struggle for civil rights, and, ultimately, the movement against the Vietnam War.

A.J. Muste at a rally opposing the Vietnam War: His anti-war action during World War I had cost him his ministry at the time, but it had opened the door to his future development.
photo credit: Swarthmore College Peace Collection

Perhaps the most dramatic shift from theory into action was that of W.E.B. DuBois. For years he had worked in academia where "I tried to isolate myself in the ivory tower of race." As a scientist he had broken new ground, developing the new science of sociology and applying it for the first time to the Negro race, but his work was having no effect in the real world. It was only when his "indignation overflowed" that he turned to "aggressive action" and called a conference of activists that met near Niagara Falls. That started the Niagara Movement which then became the NAACP (National Association for Advancement of Colored People) where DuBois became a leading activist for civil rights and later for peace.

It is a basic principle of the new psychology that people are transformed by the actions that they initiate. Not only the consequences of the actions, but the very process of taking action changes the actor so that he or she becomes a "new person" operating at a higher level of consciousness. Values and purpose are reinforced. Anger is channeled into activity, rather than turned inward and allowed to fester into pessimism. Pessimism is dispelled by real results. As Sandy Pollack wrote, "I have to work for what I want, and that's where the beauty and joy lies...when I'm engaged in 'struggle,' in accomplishing anything of any sort, I'm not depressed - but feel rather good."

People are transformed by their actions whether or not the actions are successful. If the actions are successful, activists learn that it is possible for an individual to influence the course of history, as Helen Caldicott has put it:

> Many seem to believe that it has simply become impossible for an individual to influence the course of national and world events. I disagree. My experience in Australia from 1971 to 1976 taught me that democracy can still be made to work - that by exerting electoral pressure, an aroused citizenry can still move its government

to the side of morality and common sense. In fact, the momentum for movement in this direction can only originate in the heart and mind of the individual citizen. Moreover, it takes only one person to initiate the process, and that person may be politically naive and inexperienced, just as I was when I first spoke out.

Unsuccessful actions can also play a positive role if they are assessed correctly and the struggle is shifted to a higher level. At a lower level, the struggle may run into problems caused by a higher level of the system, and only by shifting to a higher level of action can these problems be overcome. No one illustrates this more clearly than Eugene Victor Debs. His American Railway Union was able to win "clear and complete" in the initial phases of their strike, but then the government joined with the corporations to defeat the strike. Only by shifting the attack to the capitalist system itself could this be overcome:

> At this juncture there was delivered, from wholly unexpected quarters, a swift succession of blows....an army of detectives was equipped with badge and beer and bludgeon and turned loose....startling rumors were set afloat; the press volleyed and thundered, and over all the wires sped the news that Chicago's white throat was in

the clutch of a red mob; injunctions flew thick and fast, arrests followed, and our office and head-quarters, the heart of the strike, was sacked, torn out and nailed up by the "lawful" authorities of the federal government....The American Railway Union was defeated but not conquered - overwhelmed but not destroyed. It lives and pulsates in the Socialist movement, and its defeat but blazed the way to economic freedom and hastened the dawn of human brotherhood.

An especially difficult psychological shift due to action can be the loss of a career, which is what occurred to A.J. Muste and Emily Balch. Although it was painful at the time, it opened the doors to their future development. For Muste, it all began when he went to an anti-war rally at the start of World War I:

I returned from the great anti-war demonstration in Washington....to lead a union Lenten service in my own church....the fact that I had gone to Washington and had not declared my support of the war on my return made me a traitor....The tension in those days was too great. I resigned. Almost without exception, in World War I, pacifist ministers lost their pulpits, or, as in Seattle....the minister "kept his pulpit but lost his congregation."

Emily Balch accepted an invitation to sail across the Atlantic with an anti-war group of prominent American women to meet their European counterparts opposed to World War I which was raging at the time:

> Although they did not know it, the lives of several of the women on board the Noordam were to be completely changed by the trip. Jane Addams was to lose her tremendous national prestige, to regain it only in the course of time. Emily Balch was to forfeit her professorship, and her means of livelihood. Both were to be drawn into a new career, into international political work....And finally, to crown their pioneering though unspectacular labors, each was to receive the accolade of the Nobel Peace Prize.

Not all transformations are so dramatic; instead, each small step of action may lead to another, until one becomes deeply involved. For Bertrand Russell, on the eve of World War I, his first action was to circulate a petition against the war, then write a letter-to-the-editor, then to attend anti-war meetings, and finally "I gave practically my whole time and energies to the affairs of the conscientious objectors." Similarly, Helen Caldicott describes how her involvement began with a simple act:

I began by writing a letter to a local newspaper. That letter generated some supportive correspondence, and a TV news program asked me to comment on the medical hazards posed by fallout.   France had tested another nuclear device, and planned to detonate four more in the next few months. Each time the French tested a bomb, I appeared on television again, explaining the dangers of radiation. As the public became better informed, a movement to stop the French tests coalesced around the medical facts.

Other steps in consciousness development such as affiliation, personal integration and world-historic consciousness tend to come after the initial step of action rather than before it.   Since this is not immediately obvious, it is worth considering this fact in the words from the oral history of a local peace activist:

When people look back over several decades, they tend to make more of a unity out of their lives than they might actually have had at the time, especially in this country where politics has been such an on and off thing since World War II. I think that a lot of us acted first and thought later. So later you say, "Oh, I see how everything fit together...." None of our activity came out of Marxism, socialism, or any kind of traditional radicalism at all. It was later that I began to learn about those things to see if I could theorize what I'd experienced in practice.

One source of evidence that higher steps of consciousness come later than action, rather than before it, comes from the fact that initial action for peace and justice often begins at a young age. Sandy Pollack was a teenager when she first became active:

> On a winter Sunday the adults in her life met to discuss picketing at several high schools, including Sandy's, against military recruitment by the ROTC. Sandy listened, but was quiet and no one noticed her. Cecelia and Harry, driving past her school early the next morning, were therefore surprised to see their daughter carrying a picket sign, with three adults, half-frozen in the winter damp. Sandy was beginning to shape her own life. She was acting not from a sense of "responsibility," but from a dawning sense of power, that one person's acts could, in fact, make an enormous difference.

Dorothy Day was 19 when she set forth on her own in New York to find a job and an apartment and ended up working for the New York **Call**, a socialist paper that engaged her fully in the peace and justice movements of the crucial years around World War I. And Eugene Victor Debs was 19 when he joined the newly formed lodge of the Brotherhood of Locomotive Firemen in his home town and he was immediately chosen as its secretary. "Day and night I worked for the brotherhood," he wrote, and within three years he was chosen associate editor of their national magazine.

Action is the key that unlocks the door to higher levels of consciousness development. Through action one is led to affiliate with organizations where action can be collectively planned and effectively carried out. It is action that forces one to reorganize and integrate one's social relations around the issues of peace and justice. It is only through action that one can achieve world-historic consciousness. An armchair theorist can read and think all he wants, but without the test of practice and the collective wisdom of organizational action and assessment of that action, the armchair theorist will simply spin abstract ideas that diverge further and further from the real course of history.

AFFILIATION VS. ANARCHISM AND INDIVIDUALISM

We don't need any special psychological principle to explain why activists move on to the step of affiliation: quite simply they find that the power of their action is greater when they work in a group rather than alone. As Debs concluded at the end of his life, "Unorganized you are helpless, you are held in contempt. Power comes through unity."

Affiliation is not just a practical matter; it produces a psychological transformation. Purpose becomes shared. Anger is collectivized. Action becomes not only effective, but also more complex, with a division of labor. With all of this there comes a profound psychological change, as Martin Luther King Jr. has eloquently described:

> If anybody had told me a couple of years ago, when I accepted the presidency of the Mississippi Improvement Association, that I would be in this position, I would have avoided it with all my strength. This is not the life I expected to lead. But gradually you take some responsibility, then a little more, until finally you are not in control anymore. You have to give

yourself entirely. Then, once you make up your mind that you **are** giving yourself, then you are prepared to do anything that serves the Cause and advances the Movement. I have reached that point. I have no option any more about what I will do. I have given myself fully.

Debs, in his eloquent style, makes a similar observation about his affiliation in the Socialist Party:

The little that I am, the little that I am hoping to be, I owe to the Socialist movement. It has given me my ideas and ideals; my principles and convictions, and I would not exchange one of them for all of Rockefeller's blood-stained dollars. It has taught me how to serve - a lesson to me of priceless value. It has taught me the ecstacy in the handclasp of a comrade. It has enabled me....to take my place side by side with you in the great struggle for the better day.

And Emily Balch put it quite simply that her affiliation with the Women's International League for Peace and Freedom gave her "great exhilaration in the sense of active and organized comradeship with women working for peace all over the world." Affiliation provides not only inspiration, but it also provides a necessary psychological support to initiate and sustain difficult actions. For example, after being fired from his job as a minister, A.J. Muste joined "a group of radical Christian pacifists who were loosely associated in what we called The Comradeship." Stimulated by a group discussion that "somehow we had to translate the ideal of brotherhood into reality," Muste and other members of the Comradeship involved themselves in the difficult Lawrence textile strike of 1919:

> The fellowship among us was constant. There was never the slightest doubt that our families would be taken care of if any of us were injured or failed. In the feverish atmosphere of a mass strike, amidst the practical decisions that had to be made daily about matters in which we had no previous experience and which involved "compromises" of a kind which would never arise in an intentional community, we were, on the one hand, under a real, though not externally imposed, discipline of the group and on the other hand, materially and spiritually sustained by that fellowship.

Jane Addams and Emily Green Balch, Nobel prize winners (8th and 9th from left). They found "great exhilaration in the sense of active and organized commitment with women working for peace all over the world."

photo credit: Swarthmore College Peace Collection

Once a person has affiliated, the same psychological process, previously internal, that led that person to join the group in the first place, now becomes externalized into the process of recruiting others. As an organizer Jane Addams was unmatched. Starting from her affiliation at Hull House that was "held together in that soundest of all social bonds, the companionship of mutual interests," Jane Addams and her colleagues established a network of organizations ranging from neighborhood cooperatives and clubs to national and international organizations that endure to the present day, including the League of Women Voters, American Civil Liberties Union, and the Women's International League for Peace and Freedom. Sandy Pollack who joined the

Communist Party when she was only 19, was apparently a remarkable organizer as well, as described in this fragment of a poem by her husband:

> My wife knitted united fronts, endured acid meetings, bore calumny, but wherever she worked, groups went from smaller to larger.

The largest of these groups, the June 12 demonstration of 1982, numbered over one million people, the largest peace demonstration in U.S. history. Seeing the size of the crowd, she asked, "What're we going to do next? How about a coordinated world-wide action?"

More than any other step of consciousness development, affiliation requires the learning of psychological skills. There are positive skills to be developed such as the patience of a Pollack, the willingness to compromise and accept group discipline of a Muste, and the courageous generosity of Martin Luther King Jr. The great skill of Jane Addams was not only critical to the success of the Hague Conference that brought together women from both sides during World War I, but it also served as an inspiration to Emily Balch, who described it as follows:

> Difficult as it is to conduct business with so mixed and differing a constituency, with different languages, different rules of parliamentary procedure, and divergent views, Miss Addams and the other officials carried on orderly and effective sessions, marked by the most active will for unity that I have ever felt in an assemblage.

Affiliation also requires the overcoming of negative habits. W.E.B. DuBois, faced with the task of organizing the Niagara Movement, recalled that he was ill-equipped for his first major organizing role:

> I was no natural leader of men. I could not slap people on the back and make friends of strangers. I could not easily break down an inherited reserve; or at all times curb a biting critical tongue. Nevertheless, having put my hand to the plow, I had to go on.

For the most part the negative qualities that hinder affiliation are not inherited, but are due to the lack of training for cooperation in Western society. After meeting and working with Peter Maurin, whose watchword was "community," Dorothy Day became acutely aware of our society's failing:

> Man is not made to live alone. We all recognized that truth. But we were not truly communitarian, Peter said - we were only gregarious, as most people in cities are. Peter knew that most of us not only had not been trained to disciplined work, but we did not know how to work together.

Given his background in the world of academics, which encourages competition and individualism from the first grade on, it is not surprising that Bertrand Russell found it particularly difficult to affiliate:

> Throughout my life I have longed to feel that oneness with large bodies of human beings that is experienced by the members of enthusiastic crowds. The longing has often been strong enough to lead me into self deception. I have imagined myself in turn a Liberal, a Socialist, or a Pacifist, but I have never been any of these things, in any profound sense. Always the sceptical intellect, when I have most wished it silent, has whispered doubts to me, has cut me off from the facile enthusiasms of others, and has transported me into a desolate solitude.

The negative tendencies of individualism such as those taught in the universities, can lead to anarchism in practice. The organizing of Helen Caldicott exemplifies this tendency, as she describes the "loose knit organizations" she formed while still in Australia:

> Although we met once a week to report on what we had all been doing, there were no rules and few agendas. Each individual was totally free to do what he or she considered necessary to further the cause. The organization imposed no restraints....

Later, when she came to the United States, Caldicott apparently found it difficult to work with already established organizations, and instead she founded her own group called WAND. Russell's reluctance to affiliate became a matter of great historical importance when, almost 90 years old, he split from the Campaign for Nuclear Disarmament that he had previously helped to establish, and he formed, instead, the Committee of 100 dedicated to civil disobedience. According to biographer Ronald Clark, Russell got a reputation "for abandoning campaigns when they reached the crest of the wave."

There is a special risk related to affiliation - the risk of sectarianism. If the analysis of the group that one has joined turns out to be sectarian, in other words, narrow and isolated from the common people and the course of history, then one's work becomes ineffective. At best, a sectarian group may be irrelevant, and, at worst, it may be counterproductive to the progress of peace and justice. In such a case, the activist is faced with the difficult necessity of changing the direction of the group or leaving it and affiliating with another.

Despite its risks, there is no substitute for affiliation in the development of consciousness. The isolated individual, no matter how brilliant, is incapable of making history. Only through affiliation and leadership in organizations can a person develop world-historic consciousness. We will return to this question after dealing with the next step of personal integration.

PERSONAL INTEGRATION VS. BURNOUT

To sustain action and affiliation, these steps must be integrated with an activist's other social relations, including family, friendships, and means of earning a living. The question of personal integration is especially important because it enables an activist to sustain a lifetime of involvement and to avoid the danger of burnout.

The danger of burnout is especially great for peace

and justice activists because more than others, they are con fronted by deliberate pressures from the forces of militarism and exploitation. These pressures can be overwhelming such as those that led to the assassination of Martin Luther King, Jr. Most major peace activists have been under attack by the police and mass me59dia, and many have been sent to prison at one time or another. The pressure intensifies at certain periods of history:

A.J. Muste and Dorothy Day join in a draft-card burning to protest the war in Vietnam: "We must have a community, a group, an exchange with others."

Photo credit: Tom Cornell, Ben Fernandez and the Marquette University Library

Thus, for example, it is not accidental that during World War I when Eugene Victor Debs, Dorothy Day and Bertrand Russell were imprisoned and Emily Balch and A.J. Muste lost their jobs, that Debs, Day, Russell, and Jane Addams all had physical and nervous breakdowns.

Sustaining a lifetime of personal action and involvement requires a network of social support. Thus, for example, despite the great pressures against him, Martin Luther King Jr. was able to sustain his work with the help of his "ground crew." This included not only his wife Coretta and the rest of his immediate family, but also their church, the Ebenezer Baptist in Atlanta:

> His wonderful Ebenezer family had encouraged him and given him and his organization unstinted support during all the difficult years of his struggle. They were truly what he referred to as "the ground crew." Without them doing their job in the background, in a very big way, he could not have given to the nation and the world the kind of leadership he did.

In many ways, King's "ground crew" was ideal. In addition to the new support he obtained for civil rights action in the Montgomery community, not to mention around the world, he could integrate this with a loving and supportive family, a salary from the church, and the support of his past activities (academic work) and affiliations (the church). However, they did not all immediately support his broadening the commitment to oppose the war in Vietnam, and for that support it was necessary for him and Coretta to struggle.

Eugene Victor Debs was able to sustain his lifelong commitment with the support of a network similar to King's "ground crew." As biographer Ray Ginger points out, the following description by Debs of his wife's support could also describe the support from his parents, his brother Theodore, and his brother-in-law Arthur Baur:

> She shared what came in stormy days without complaint, and when I returned after many weeks of weary travel she had the home sweet and cozy and ministered to me in all tenderness until I was rested and refreshed for another journey....For years she was our secretary of state. She wrote all my letters in long hand before the days of the typewriter, and I had a large correspondence. She trudged through the snow to a cold office when I was out on the road, lighted the fire, emptied the ashes, cleaned the office, answered the mail, shipped bundles of literature to me and to others, and then returned to cook her meals, set the house in order, and attend to the wants of the home.

For Debs, like King, the key question was whether the support network continued to support him when he broadened the scope of his commitment from trade unionism to socialism around 1896 and again to his opposition to World War I in 1917. According to the Ginger biography the immediate family of Debs, as well as many of his trade union comrades, supported his move to socialism. But when he opposed World War I, he found himself without such support, which may help to explain why he was "hesitant and floundering," in "ill-health," and "groping in the dark," in the months before he gave his famous anti-war speech in Canton, Ohio, for which he was arrested, tried and imprisoned.

To sustain the struggle, activists must share the burden of political responsibility with other people in their organizations - developing relationships of mutual support. Otherwise, the whole "burden of the world" seems to sit on their shoulders alone, and eventually the stress becomes too much for a single individual to take. Apparently, this is what caused Helen Caldicott to announce, at the 1985 national conference of WAND, that she was retiring from her active leadership of the organization she had founded:

I've been working for 16 years....travelling all the time, sleeping in strange beds, giving two or three speeches in a day, dealing with the press all day, having to give a speech and arouse an audience enough to make them cry and change their lives that night or that day. I dream about it every night, as I'm sure many of you do. And I wake up in a cold sweat, frightened, anxious, guilty. I feel the whole world is on my shoulders. Well, that's right. I should feel that, but I'm sinking into it. I'm drowning in it. I have to stop.

"Burnout" is not just the absence of the feeling of social support, but it is also a particular psychological state that may deepen by degrees into depression with inactivity, disaffiliation, despair, debauchery, guilt, exhaustion, nervous and physical illness. All of these symptoms are described by Dorothy Day in her description of her "long loneliness." The psychological processes by which the phases of depression lead deeper and deeper, like a vicious circle, are not yet well understood scientifically. No doubt, as I have written in a technical article, they include profound hormone changes that transform the entire physiological response to social situations.[11]

In describing her "long loneliness," Dorothy Day is quite explicit about the social causes and the integrative cure that was needed:

I was lonely, deadly lonely. And I was to find out then, as I found out so many times, over and over again, that women especially are social beings, who are not content with just husband and family, but must have a community, a group, an exchange with others.

"Just husband" for Dorothy Day was Forster, with whom she had a common law marriage and a child named Tamar. But Forster did not support her activity, because he was an anarchist whose anger was turned inward rather than being used to stimulate action (see quotation on page 16). Finally, Dorothy Day met Peter Maurin and together they built the kind of community she was looking for. Maurin aroused "a sense of your own capacities for work, for accomplishment." Maurin called it "a synthesis of 'cult, culture, and cultivation.'" For Dorothy Day, it meant the synthesis of all her past actions and affiliations: social activism, journalistic work, a family, and Roman Catholic affiliation.

Personal integration provides not only practical support, but it also produces an enriching and rewarding psychological transformation. By integrating each new affiliation with their previous networks of personal relationships and group affiliations, King, Debs, and Day (after meeting Maurin) were able to grow not just in public stature and strength, but also in private individuality. They were not "swallowed up" by their new affiliations and did not lose their individuality in any nightmare such as the fear of "enthusiastic crowds" that prevented Bertrand Russell from taking the step of affiliation. Instead, through affiliations they developed even more unique personalities.

When organizations such as religious and political cults discourage the personal integration of their members, they contribute to the myth that affiliation requires persons to lose their individuality. The extreme case is the deperson-alization process of the U.S. Army by which they "break in" new recruits by stripping them of all personal relationships and affiliations and putting them into a standard uniform. Many religious and political cults that have sprung up in recent years engage in similar depersonalization procedures. There is a danger that organizations in the peace movement may adopt such methods which, in the long run, weaken rather than strengthen the new recruits. For example, there was Muste's dream for the "Comradeship" that envisioned "the formation of a band of evangels, patterned partly after the original Christians....cut loose....from the existing order....

dressing uniformly (though not 'too much like a military uniform or clerical dress') to symbolize their internal unity and their repudiation of the world." It is not surprising, given such a vision, that Muste later in life fell victim to sectarianism, in which his analysis became narrow and out of touch with the historical movement of the times.

One method that the State uses to repress movements for peace and justice is to outlaw organizations and force the membership underground where personal integration is much more difficult to achieve. For example, in the biography of Sandy Pollack, one misses any description of the struggle it must have been for her to integrate her affiliation with the Communist Party, which must have been secret to some extent, with all of her other social relations. The tension of such a struggle may help explain why it is that she blossomed after she began to work internationally in solidarity movements with Cuba and Nicaragua where she could be openly proud of being a Communist.

The repression of sexuality in our society makes personal integration more difficult. This is such a problem that the profession of psychoanalysis has developed largely to deal with it. The personal costs of society's sexual repression have been described well by W.E.B. DuBois:

> On one aspect of my life, I look back upon with mixed feelings: and that is on matters of friendship and sex ....Indeed the chief blame which I lay on my New England schooling was the inexcusable ignorance of sex....In my hometown sex was deliberately excluded from talk and if possible from thought....As teacher in the rural districts of East Tennessee, I was literally raped by the unhappy wife who was my landlady. From that time through my college course at Harvard and my study in Europe, I went through a desperately recurring fight to keep the sex instinct in control. A brief trial with prostitution in Paris affronted my sense of decency. I lived more or less regularly with a shop girl in Berlin, but was ashamed. Then when I returned home to teach, I was faced with the connivance of certain fellow teachers at adultery with their wives. I was literally frightened into marriage before I was able to support a family.

The cost of sexual repression helps explain why DuBois' marriage of 53 years was not well integrated with his political development. Instead, "it suffered from the fundamental drawback of modern American marriage: a difference in aim and function between its partners." And the repression of sexual-ity in our culture also helps to explain why DuBois was led to make a serious mistake when he dismissed "a young man, long my disciple and student, then my co-helper and successor to part of my work" because he was arrested for homosexual behavior. Afterwards, DuBois "spent heavy days regretting my act."

Both Jane Addams and Emily Balch may have been hampered in their attempts to achieve personal integration of their anti-war work by the repressive attitudes about sexuality, including homosexuality, in our society. Both were victims of burnout. When Jane Addams was attacked viciously by the press for her opposition to World War I, abandoned by many of her friends from social work, she fell ill and suffered from "three years of semi-invalidism" and "a bald sense of social opprobrium....very near to self-pity." And Emily Balch suffered from nervous fatigue which forced her to interrupt her work for long periods. Although each had the support of a close woman companion, Mary Rozet Smith in the case of Jane Addams and Helen Cheever in the case of Emily Balch, it seems likely that prevailing sexual mores may have limited the extent to which they could be fully integrated into their life. Emily Balch regretted having only "the half-life of the unmarried woman." Whether or not their relationships were homosexual (and we may never know), they could not be made public and thereby integrated with their political lives. As their mutual friend Alice Hamilton explained to a biographer of Addams, such topics were not discussed in those days, and "the very fact that I would bring the subject up was an indication of the separation between my generation and hers."

The work of earning a living is transformed when it becomes integrated into work for peace and justice. Raising money for the "movement" is not the same as raising it for yourself and your family. It is removed from the private, "selfish" domain of capitalist society, into the unselfish, collective domain and becomes a part of one's political work. Dorothy Day describes how, after founding the Catholic Worker, she took to the road to seek contributions to keep the paper in print. And Helen Caldicott describes how, after joining the physician's movement, she would approach her physician colleagues at meetings to sign petitions and give one dollar so that the petition could be published.

For most people, including many activists for peace and justice, the step of personal integration is the highest step of consciousness development. But the peace movement needs leadership and for that a higher step of consciousness is needed, world-historic consciousness.

WORLD-HISTORIC CONSCIOUSNESS VS. SECTARIANISM

World-historic consciousness, the highest step of consciousness, is not the quality of an individual acting alone, but of a leader working in affiliation. It is the kind of leadership that enables action and affiliation for peace and justice to develop in an effective and progressive rather than a narrow and sectarian direction. It's the ability of a leader to know the mood of the people, to analyze the strengths and directions of all political forces, and to organize and broaden the political character of the movement so that it is in step with the agenda of history, which, in the present time, means the abolition of war.

First of all, a leader must know the mood of the people. This can come only from long and direct experience working among them. The leadership of Eugene Victor Debs came from such experience:

> I had fired an engine and been stung by the exposure and hardship of the rail. I was with the boys in their weary watches, at the broken engine's side and often helped to bear their bruised and bleeding bodies back to wife and child again. How could I but feel the burden of their wrongs? How could the seed of agitation fail to take deep root in my heart?

Her years of service among the people enabled Jane Addams to play a leading role in the peace movement:

> ....in every social grade and class in the whole circle of genuine occupations there are mature men and women of moral purpose and specialized knowledge, who because they have become efficient unto life, may contribute an enrichment to the pattern of human culture....he who would incorporate these experiences into the common heritage must....be equipped with a wide and familiar acquaintance with the human spirit and its productions.

Second, a leader must understand the strengths and directions of all political forces in a systemic, not a superficial way. Such understanding must be "radical" - it must go to the roots of things - their economic and social causes. It must not be content with talk of superficial change, but must recognize that peace requires fundamental economic and political changes in society. In the words of Emily Balch:

> When war came in 1914 I felt this at first mainly as a senseless interruption of social-economic progress. I felt that war must be got rid of so that the threat of war might not interrupt and distort the course of this progress. Only

gradually I came to understand at least partly how deeply war is intertwined with our whole economic and social system, our scale of values, our ideas of what is right and of supreme importance. I see no chance of social progress apart from fundamental changes on both the economic and the political side, replacing national anarchy by organized cooperation of all peoples to further their common interest, and replacing economic anarchy, based on the search for personal profit, by a great development of the cooperative spirit.

Martin Luther King, Jr. pickets with striking chemical workers: "Let us be dissatisfied until every man can have food and material necessities."

photo credit: Schomburg Center of New York Public Library

In retrospect, Eugene Debs realized that such a radical perspective was missing in his ill-fated keadership of the American Railway Union.

> My supreme conviction was that if the railroad men were only organized in every branch of the service and all acted together in concert they could redress their wrongs and regulate the conditions of their employment ....I had yet to learn the workings of the capitalist system, the resources of its masters and the weakness of its slaves....It all seems very strange to me now, taking a backward look, that my vision was so focalized on a single objective point that I utterly failed to see what now appears as clear as the noonday sun.....

World-historic consciousness requires what Helen Caldicott has called, "a global view of reality and a sense of moral responsibility for humanity's future." Jane Addams called it "a new consciousness, a nascent world consciousness:"

> But whether we care for it or not, our own experiences are more and more influenced by the experiences of widely scattered people; the modern world is developing an almost mystical consciousness of the continuity and interdependence of mankind. There is a lively

sense of the unexpected and yet inevitable action and reaction between ourselves and all the others who happen to be living upon the planet at the same moment. Perhaps no presentation is so difficult as that which treats of the growth of a new consciousness....this nascent world consciousness....

As Emily Balch puts it, this global view of reality is not a view of what already exists, but a "trend of development" towards "a planetary civilization:"

In looking back over the years, I have not the feeling that our efforts have been unreasonable. On the contrary, I have the impression that although the world was not ready to realize them, the trend of development runs obviously and unmistakably toward the end that we have sought - a planetary civilization.

In the development of a world-historic consciousness, one important factor is world travel in which the travel is used as a means to study and reflect both upon the direction of world events and the means of achieving social change at home. As DuBois recalls:

The most important work of the decade as I now look back upon it was my travel. Before 1918 I had made three trips to Europe; but now between 1918 and 1928 I made four trips of extraordinary meaning: to France directly after the close of the war and during the Congress of Versailles; to England, Belgium, France and Geneva in the earliest days of the League of Nations; to Spain, Portugal and Africa in 1923 and 1924; and to Germany, Russia and Constantinople in 1926. I could scarcely have encompassed a more vital part of the modern world picture than in those stirring journeys. They gave me a depth of knowledge and a breath of view which was of incalculable value for realizing and judging modern conditions, and above all the problem of race in America.

World-historic consciousness is a result of struggle on ever-widening planes of significance, as the development of the individual becomes increasingly enmeshed with the development of all humanity. In describing the development of Martin Luther King Jr., his wife, Coretta, compares it to a scroll unfolding:

When Martin got the Nobel Prize...then, when he made the statement on Vietnam, I had the strong feeling that this was the beginning of a larger work for him which would develop into something greater than we could conceive at the time. All along in our struggle one phase had led to another. As the years unfolded, it was like watching a scroll unfolding, you see more and more as you unroll it. There was a pattern and a process at work for the development of mankind.

For King, there was a progression from one plane of work on civil rights on behalf of Afro-Americans, to a broader plane for justice for the working class (he was killed in Memphis where he was speaking on behalf of the garbage workers strike which he characterized as "not a race war, it is now a class war"), to the broadest plane of all, his opposition to the Vietnam War and advocacy of peace and freedom for all the peoples of the world.

King's tribute to the world-historic consciousness of DuBois, on the 100th anniversary of his birth, could as well have been a tribute to King himself:

> In conclusion let me say that Dr. DuBois' greatest virtue was his committed empathy with all the oppressed and his divine dissatisfaction with all forms of injustice. Today we are still challenged to be dissatisfied. Let us be dissatisfied until every man can have food and material necessities for his body, culture and education for his mind, freedom and human dignity for his spirit...Let us be dissatisfied until our brother of the Third World - Asia, Africa and Latin America - will no longer be the victim of imperialist exploitation, but will be lifted from the long night of poverty, illiteracy and disease. Let us be dissatisfied until this pending cosmic elegy will be transformed into a creative

psalm of peace and "justice will roll down like waters from a mighty stream."

For DuBois, the journey towards world-historic consciousness led him from one plane of action to another. He overcame a narrow, sectarian view confined to the question of race relations (he supported World War I because it was a chance to advance Afro-Americans as military officers), and he achieved a mature consciousness that included the entire world and all races within its scope:

> I wavered for years, advocating socialism first as a racial program; then as a national effort and after this trip of 1958 as a definite and direct step to join the world movement toward a socialism leading toward communism, and embracing the colored world and that part of the white world willing to give up colonialism and private capitalism. But, as I say, this decision was slow in the making.

For recognizing and acting upon the fact that socialism had become the leading force for peace (DuBois was responsible for leading the drive to collect millions of U.S. signatures on the Stockholm Peace Appeal), he was put on trial at the age of 83 as an "agent" of the Soviet Union. DuBois' vision went far beyond that of his critics, however, as he foresaw not only the leading role for peace played by the socialist countries, but also the important role for peace that would be played by the emerging non-aligned movement:

> ....Pan-Africa, working together through its independent units, should seek to develop a new African economy and cultural center standing between Europe and Asia, taking from and contributing to both. It should stress peace and join no military alliance and refuse to fight for settling European quarrels....should try to build a socialism founded on old African communal life...in peaceful cooperation and without presuming to dictate as to how Socialism must or can be attained at particular times and places.

As DuBois progressed in the development of his world- historic consciousness, he was forced to leave the organization that he had founded 25 years earlier, the National Association for Advancement of Colored People:

> No sooner had I come to this conclusion [the necessity of socialism] than I saw that I was out of touch with my organization and that the question of leaving it was only a matter of time.

DuBois illustrates a most important truth that can be quite painful in its operation: that consciousness development, in order to avoid sectarianism, often requires one to leave organizations with narrow perspectives and to seek out new affiliations with a broader view.

Eugene Victor Debs (center) receiving the Presidential nomination in 1920 from a Socialist Party delegation while he was imprisoned for opposing World War I.
Photo credit: Tamiment Library of New York University

Eugene Victor Debs progressed from one plane of activity to another in much the same way as DuBois, widening its scope until it encompassed the whole world. Debs began with a narrow sectarian view of labor federations, first only the locomotive firemen, then all the railroad workers, then all the working class, and finally came to a political commitment to socialism as a system of peace and justice for all people in the world (see quotation on page 21). Just as DuBois did not develop his analysis in isolation, but in dialogue with the Communist Party, so Debs developed his analysis in affiliation with the Socialist Party of his day.

For Sandy Pollack a vision came from a visit to Cuba:

> Perhaps more than any other single event, that visit to Cuba in November 1969 on the first Venceremos Brigade focused the rest of her life....Sandy saw that socialism was possible, could be successful. She could see it, touch it, examine it....It was tangible; it could work.

For world-historic consciousness one does not have to become a socialist or communist, but one must work with them. One must recognize them as powerful allies in the present struggle against war and that they help provide a concrete vision for a future peaceful world. Anti-communism is the most destructive form of sectarianism. It weakens the unity that needed for strength and the vision needed for inspiration. Martin Luther King Jr. recognized this fact. Although he was not a communist, himself, King acknowledged that DuBois was a "radical all of his life" and "some people would like to ignore the fact that he was a Communist in his later years." King concluded that "our irrational obsessive anti-communism has led us into too many quagmires to be retained as if it were a mode of scientific thinking [10].

Of course, not every activist rises to the step of world-historic consciousness. For example, despite the great intellectual talents of Bertrand Russell, his temperamental inability to affiliate stunted his development and kept him from working with groups where he could have developed world-historic consciousness. Instead, the older he grew, the more cynical he became:

> The way in which the world has developed during the last fifty years has brought about in me changes opposite to those which are supposed to be typical of old age. One is frequently assured by men who have no doubt of their own wisdom that old age should bring serenity and a larger vision in which seeming evils are viewed as means to ultimate good. I cannot accept any such view.

It is ironic that Russell should blame "the way in which the world has developed" rather than the way in which he himself developed for the failure to achieve a "larger vision." Dorothy Day also failed to achieve a world-h9istoric vision. In her preface to **The Long Loneliness** she asks "What is man, where is he going, what is his destiny?" and answers, "It is a mystery. We are sons of God, and 'it is a terrible thing to fall into the hands of the living God.'" She concludes that in her life, "I feel that I have done nothing well." Such a conclusion is quite similar to the one that Bertrand Russell came to: "I cannot pretend that what I have done in regard to social and political problems has had any great importance." In each case, it was impossible for them to appreciate the great importance of their work because they lacked the world-historic consciousness with which to evaluate it.

The failure of Russell and Day to achieve world-historic consciousness had serious historical consequences. Although both ended up playing progressive roles in opposing the Vietnam War, each played a reactionary role with respect to the rise of the Cold War. Bertrand Russell's anti-communism led him for several years to work for British Cold War propaganda agencies and even to publicly advocate a nuclear attack upon the Soviet Union. Later on, however, he reversed his position and the

Russell-Einstein manifesto of 1955 set the stage for the first East-West scientific cooperation for peace, the Pugwash Conference of 1957

Dorothy Day became caught up in the contradictory approaches of the catholics and communists; although she made a personal integration in her own life, she could not resolve the historical contradictions between them. As a result, she had a major negative impact on the Cold War, without even having to take a public position concerning it. The Association of Catholic Trade Unionists, which grew out of a study group she had started at the Catholic Worker in the depression years, developed into a sectarian organization that attacked communists in the trade unions. They were largely responsible for destroying the labor involvement of the CIO in the peace movement during the critical early years of the Cold War. As I recount in **The American Peace Movements** (see footnote 3), the Association did....

> "its utmost to turn the key Catholic CIO leaders.... into anti-Communists." The Catholic attack on the labor movement was carried out by spies, informers, infiltrators, and "ACT" cells" in the CIO that were "pledged to keep Communists out" of key areas in the labor movement. Once the CIO withdrew its

organized labor support, the Wallace campaign had no chance of victory.

The defeat of the Wallace campaign not only ended mass opposition to the Cold War, but it also led into the period of McCarthyism, the worst period in U.S. peace movement history.

Sectarianism can take various forms, although in today's world, sectarianism is usually marked by anti-communism in one form or another. Taking up the cause of nonviolent opposition to U.S. racism and nuclear weapons in the 1960's, A.J. Muste remarked that:

> we are not any longer a sectarian - using the term in a good sense - movement, existing apart from the main political decisions and affecting them only in a very long-range and indirect sense. We now function in mass movements.

But Muste learned of sectarianism from bitter experience. During the 1930's, while most of the peace movement was joining together to fight against the rise of fascism, Muste took what he later called a "detour" into work with a small radical sect of Trotskyites, which, under his leadership, came to be called "Musteites." And after World War II, caught in the quagmire of anti-communism, he refused to take part in the greatest attempt to stop the Cold War, the Progressive Party campaign for Wallace in 1948, because of what he perceived as its "heavy Communist influence." Later, however, during the Vietnam War, Muste overcame sectarianism and played a major role in refusing to exclude Leftist groups and welcoming all organizations into the growing anti-war coalition.

World-historic consciousness brings history and psychology together into an inseparable unity. In contrast to the individualist approach that consider freedom as "freedom from the constraints of history," this approach to consciousness development sees true freedom as the freedom that comes when individuals take part in shaping the history that, in turn, shapes them. In other words, world-historic consciousness is "freedom through history." In the words of Debs, you find yourself by making history.

> You will lose nothing; you will gain everything.
> Not only will you lose nothing but you will find
> something of infinite value, and that something
> will be yourself. And that is your supreme need -
> to find yourself - to really know yourself and
> your purpose in life. You need to know that it is
> your duty to rise above the animal plane of

existence. You need to know that it is for you to know something about literature and science and art. You need to know that you are verging on the edge of a great new world.

At the end of the speech, which is the speech for which he was tried and imprisoned because he called for non-cooperation with World War I, Debs called upon his listeners "to build the new nation and the free republic. We need industrial and social builders. We Socialists are the builders of the beautiful world that is to be."

The freedom of world-historic consciousness is also a burden, because it is the quality of leadership rather than the quality of an individual. The leader is responsible to all who look to him or her for leadership, which can be a heavy and difficult responsibility. Coretta Scott King describes the burden that the Nobel Peace Prize placed upon her husband:

What was the deeper meaning of all this - some meaning that we were not yet able to understand? For this was not just a prize for civil rights, but for contributing to world peace. Though we were very happy, both Martin and I realized the tremendous responsibility that this placed on him. This was, of course, the greatest recognition that had come to him, but we both knew that to accomplish what the prize really implied, we still had a long way to go. It was a great tribute, but an even more awesome burden.

World-historic consciousness corresponds to the ancient religious belief in immortality,. By engaging one's life with the development of history, the peace and justice activist becomes an integral part of an undying human tradition. In his obituary for Sandy Pollack, the Cuban ambassador to the United States, H. E. Oscar Orama expressed the form of poetry:

> Sandy
> You are tomorrow.
> You are today.
> You reached the summit of the human species
> and you will be kept alive

forever in immortal glory.

THE UNITY AND UNIVERSALITY OF
CONSCIOUSNESS DEVELOPMENT

Consciousness development is a single, unified process that reflects both the unity of the individual and the unity of human history. Although we may distinguish six discrete steps of consciousness development, we should not lose sight of the essential unity of consciousness development in the individual and its universality among all human beings. In the individual, the steps of consciousness development build upon each other so that each step is transformed by the addition of the next and no development is lost. The steps are not separate, isolated qualities, but are inter-related in the functioning of a single "person," with his or her own "personality."

In the human species, consciousness development is a shared process of all people. Our values derive from a common history, in which we are members of a vast multitude of people that extends throughout the world and that includes those who have died and those yet to be born as well as those living today. We all face a future that is increasingly tied to the future of each other. Consciousness development is not the possession of a select group of people, but is available to all who have language and membership in society. And the potential to reach the highest steps of consciousness development is available to all people, even if only attained by some.

The highest level of consciousness development comes only through the participation in the making of history, and for that reason at the present time, it can only be attained with peace activism. This is true because at the present time the achievement of peace with justice is the primary issue on the agenda of history. All other activism for social justice is related, in one way or another, to the quest for peace; it will all come to nothing if civilization goes up in the flames of nuclear war.

Today we have the opportunity to achieve a higher level of consciousness than in any previous period of history. Never before has there been such a single, universal threat to our species and such an all-inclusive, world-wide task as the task of abolishing war. Never before has our species as a whole been faced with its own ultimate question of life or death. We have come full circle: the species consciousness that gave each of us the opportunity to attain individual consciousness is now endangered; and only the full development of individual consciousness in the masses of humanity can save it.

ROOT CAUSES OF THE NEW PSYCHOLOGY

To foresee the tasks of the new psychology, we must understand its root causes. We have said that the new psychology is emerging in response to the demands of history, but history does not "cause" anything in a direct way. Instead, we must speak of a "causal chain" that begins from the economic roots of historical change. These produce political events, such as wars and revolutions, which, in turn, are the stimulus for the growth of peace movements. When peace movements

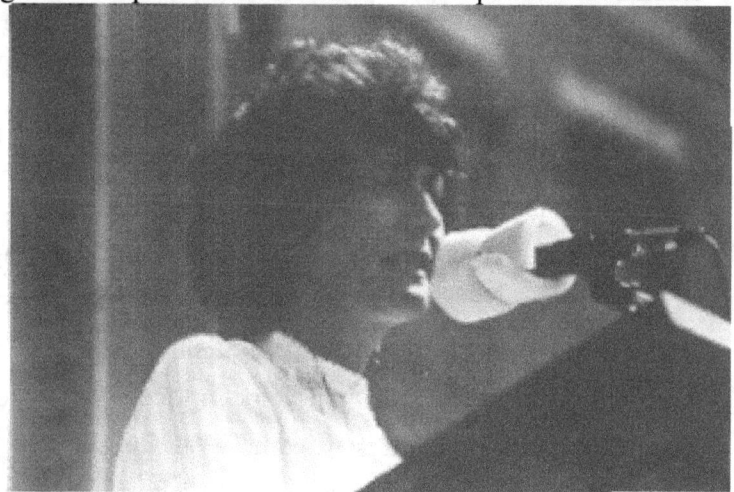

Helen Caldicott, founder of Women's Action for Nuclear Disarmament : "A global view of reality and a sense of moral responsibility for humanity's future."
Photo credit : Helen Caldicott and WAND

grow into massive size, they provide the social context for the intensification of consciousness development of individuals. Finally, it is this intensification of consciousness development that requires a new psychology.

The causal chain linking economics to wars to peace movements is documented in my book, **The American Peace Movements** (see footnote 3). The six, mass-based peace movements of U.S. history illustrate how peace movements arise in response to wars and threats of war. The Anti-Imperialist League (1898-1902) developed in response to the Spanish- American and Philippine Wars. The People's Council of America was a response to World War I (1917-1919). There were two U.S. peace movements in the 1930's in response to the rise of European fascism, the American League Against War and Fascism and the Emergency Peace Campaign. From 1946-1948 there was a mass opposition to the Cold War in the form of the Progressive Citizens of America, which sponsored the Wallace presidential campaign. In response to the Vietnam War (1966-1970) the mass peace movement was organized loosely into the "Mobes." And today, in response to the New Cold War, we have a mass peace movement associated largely with the campaign for a Nuclear Freeze. There have been many smaller peace movements, both in response to these wars and war threats, and at other times, but no others that have been able to mobilize millions of people in the United States.

The six wars and war threats that caused the mass U.S. peace movements all arose as a result of basic economic factors. These also are documented in **The American Peace Movements** and will be presented here only in outline fashion. The Philippine War and World War I were the response to economic crises of over-production and unemployment, which led the imperialist countries to increase their exploitation of poor colonial and neo-colonial countries, and which led to economic rivalry among them for these foreign markets and investment areas. These economic factors continued to play a role in causing the rise of European Fascism and World War II, as well as the Cold War and the Vietnam War, but were joined by a new factor as well: the attempt by the capitalists to reverse the shrinkage of the "free world," - i.e. the part of the world that is free for capitalist investment and exploitation. Finally, the most recent wars and war threats, culminating in today's New Cold War, are caused not only by all of the previously mentioned factors, but a new and especially powerful force: the military-industrial complex. The military-industrial complex promotes war preparation in order to profit from government orders which are free from the competition of a capitalist market.

The same economic factors that have caused wars have also caused revolutions and national liberation movements. Mass unemployment has stimulated the rise of revolutionary working class movements. The exploitation of poor colonial and neo-colonial countries has produced movements for national liberation. Both of these often take place in the ruins of capitalist countries following the devastation of inter-imperialist wars.

At one point, to many observers, socialism seemed on the way to construction a world economic system that seemed not to need war. Although the socialist countries were born through revolutionary and national liberation wars, and although they were forced to defend their revolutions militarily against invasion and attack, they avoided many of the intrinsic causes for war. Their economies were not characterized by over-production and structural unemployment. In the relations among socialist countries, there was no imperialist exploitation. To the contrary, the net flow of wealth proceeded from the richer socialist countries, towards the poorer ones [11].

Although the first edition of this book maintained that the socialist countries had escaped from the burden of a military-industrial complex, that turned out to be in error. The world was shocked at the end of the 1980's by the economic and political collapse of the Soviet Union and Eastern Europe. The collapse was caused by the overburdening of the Soviet economy with military production. Attempts to reverse the declining economy with conversion from military to civilian production were resisted by the Soviet military-industrial complex. Eventually the economy crashed and the political system collapsed on top of it.

The Soviets had tried to match the West in terms of military production, but based on an economy only half as powerful. Therefore, they were forced to invest a percentage of their science and technology that was twice as great as that of the West in their military industry. It has been estimated that 85% of all Soviet scientists, engineers and skilled workers were invested in military production, including those with the most skill as they could command higher salaries in the military sector.

By the end the Soviet economy could not produce any industrial goods of sufficient quality to export except for military and related aerospace products. Computers, machine tools, automobiles, electronic goods, clothing, all suffered from the diversion of technology, labor and raw materials to the insatiable arms race. In today's global market it is only a matter of time before such a system crashes.

The immediate effects on world peace were contradictory. On the one hand, Gorbachev and others managed a transition without repression and war, unlike what had happened after the collapse of Germany 60 years before. And major disarmament agreements were made with the West. On the other hand, the loss of socialist perspectives in the United Nations gave the West a free hand to use the UN for war-making in the Persian Gulf. And the loss of socialist support for national liberation led to defeats of progressive movements around the world.

The destruction of the socialist world resulted from a deliberate policy of the West to bankrupt them with the arms race. The long-term effects for world peace were negative, as it was interpreted as a victory for military confrontation in the West. And now there is no longer a developed alternative to the underlying causes of war - the exploitation of people within and betweeen the capitalist nations.

But the arms race is a two-edged sword. The U.S. economy is also overburdened by military production as a result of it. The U.S. is less and less able to produce quality industrial goods for export or for internal consumption [12]. It may be headed for a similar economic collapse, with political consequences that could be very dangerous for world peace.

With the end of the Cold War, the danger of inter-state wars has receded, and the danger of civil wars has become more evident. More than ever we become aware that the culture of war has always had internal as well as external aspects, that militarism has historically been used not only for war between states, but also for the maintenance of power within the state. I have documented the internal interventions of the military in U.S. history and found that there has been an average of about 20 interventions and about 12,000 troops per year for more than a century [13]. In the early years of the 19th Century, these interventions were directed primarily against native Americans and used for the maintenance of slavery. After the Civil War the interventions were used to break strikes and curb the power of trade unions. And since World War II, they have been used primarily for the control of urban riots which involve unemployed youth for the most part.

There is no reason to think that the situation in U.S history is much different from that of all the other great powers. If we are to see the replacement of the culture of war with a culture of peace, it will be necessary to replace the use and/or threat of military force for internal state control with a system of democracy which can ensure stability without coercion. This task requires an economy of peace, as well as political institutions of participative democracy.

What is needed at this point in history is the development of peace economies that are able to satisfy the needs of people without exploitation and without resort to military production. Whether this can be done at the level of the nation-state, or whether it must be accomplished at other levels, both local levels and international/regional levels, is very much a question of the day.

TASKS OF THE NEW PSYCHOLOGY

The old psychology that is taught in American universities and used to train American psychotherapists

98

is entangled, like the rest of the educational system and the mass media, in the web of militarism and inequality that pervades U.S. society. It is incapable of meeting the needs of those who are striving to translate the emerging vision of peace into reality.

The new psychology must proclaim the values of peace and justice. Its very purpose should be to promote these values in the people. This is totally unlike traditional psychology which takes a position of political "neutrality" and claims that it should not be involved

Children's march for peace on New Haven Green, October 25, 1986: "The new psychology must proclaim the values of peace and justice."

in questions of values and purpose. Practically speaking, there is no such thing as neutrality. Silence can only be interpreted as acceptance of the dominant militarism of the society. The new psychology must begin from the standpoint that its task is to oppose the values of militarism and promote the values of peace and justice. It should teach the pursuit of peace as the purpose of life.

It is not enough to stress the values of peace and justice in the family and within the circles of traditional peace and justice organizations. The new psychology should take part in the struggle to promote the values of peace and justice in the government, the mass media, and the educational systems. Whether it is the election of Congressional candidates who will speak out and work for peace, or the struggle for peace education programs in the public schools and universities, or the task of printing letters-to-editors or appearing on talk shows in order to provide an alternative to the media's militarism, the task is difficult, but ultimately necessary and rewarding. We may put ourselves in the place of the parents of a King or Pollack, the ministers of a Balch or Muste, and the teachers of an Addams or DuBois to see what the ultimate fruits can be.

The rising emphasis on values and purpose for peace comes at a time when the problem of alienation is more acute than ever for society in general and for psychology in particular. Inundated by media programs of violence, children are not sure if they will ever grow up to be adults, let alone take their part in the cycle of generations. Depression, hopelessness and despair are everywhere, and the resultant problems of suicide, drug and alcohol abuse, and criminality have reached epidemic proportions.

Anger is on the increase, fueled by increased levels of economic and political exploitation. Terrorism is also on the increase. To some extent the terrorism is conducted by the forces of militarism. But to some extent, it also comes from the accumulating anger in people who feel that have no other resort for social change. However, rather than advancing the cause of peace, terrorism victimizes the innocent and fragments the peace movement, frightening people away from activity. To reduce terrorism, the new psychology can provide an optimistic rather than pessimistic channel for the expression of anger, turning it to constructive rather than destructive action.

Many see the rise in anger as a sign for despair,

but the new psychology will see it as a force to be harnessed. However, anger is not only ignored as a positive force, but it is actively discouraged by contemporary American psychology textbooks. It is treated as if it were pathology and disease, and it is blamed for the ills of society including war and crime, while the true economic and political roots of these phenomena are hardly discussed.

It will not be enough for the new psychology to "authorize" anger. Anger is a skill that needs to be harnessed so that it is used constructively rather than destructively. When I say that "anger is the personal fuel in the social motor that resolves the institutional contradictions of history," I imply that anger is useless unless it is put into the "social motor." The new psychology must help engage people in today's "social motor," which is the peace movement, teaching them that their anger takes on constructive value within that social context. At the same time, it must guard against the harnessing of anger into reactionary social movements such as fascism.

The use of fear must not be encouraged, but must be exposed as the method of militarism and repression. The fact that fear is not an effective motivational means for changing attitudes has been known for some time by professional psychologists [15]. Instead, fear is used by those who seek to repress not only action and affiliation, but also the expression of anger. Those in the peace movement, such as Helen Caldicott, who have sought to motivate people by making them afraid of the consequences of nuclear war should reconsider their tactics lest they simply increase the feelings of helplessness and pessimism that pervade the mass media and prevent people from taking action.

The new psychology should share in the development of the emerging vision of a culture of peace. With the end of the Cold War, it may be said that such a vision is now becoming a fully developed and new step in the consciousness development of peace activists (see preface to Second Edition).

The old psychology, without the vision of a culture of peace, has been a case of the blind leading the blind. Not only does it lack vision, but it has preached pessimism. Even if war is not called "instinctive" (and sometimes the myth of the so-called "instinct for war" is actually taught in psychology courses), the old psychology teaches that personality, intelligence, sex differences, and other important personal characteristics are largely determined by genetic and early childhood factors. This gives helpless students the feeling that there is little they can accomplish by action and affiliation. This fits neatly into the pessimism of the mass media where hurricanes, plane crashes, wars, and crimes are considered "newsworthy" while organized action of peace and justice (for example, trade union actions) are censored or minimized [16].

As well as providing a concrete basis for optimism, the new psychology should directly combat the psychological warfare of pessimism. We should work to expose and eliminate the "image of the enemy" that is used to justify the arms race and isolationism which prevent cooperation with the rest of the world. We should expose and eliminate the myth of the "instinct of war" by such means as dissemination of the Seville Statement on Violence (see footnote 9). And we should take part directly in the struggle against the pessimism of the mass media, a struggle that we may expect to sharpen in the coming times.

The new psychology will be a psychology of action, unlike the old psychology that ignores action and emphasizes, instead, all kinds of passive processes. Psychology textbooks are loaded with studies of sleep and dreaming, "states of consciousness" that are considered in terms of drugs and yoga meditation, attitude change that is defined in terms of an "outside" force changing the attitudes of an otherwise passive subject, and personality traits, intelligence, and sex differences that are treated as unchanging, inherited qualities. The dominant technique of psychotherapy has been one in which the patient lies down on a couch facing away from the therapist and recalls his or her dreams and child hood experiences. How more passive can you be? Even though the practice of psychotherapy has changed in most cases, the theory derived from the old practice still dominates clinical psychology.

The new psychology must teach the skills of affiliation. From our study of autobiographies, we have seen that these skills include the willingness to compromise and accept group discipline, the courage to give of oneself and to accept criticism, while curbing the excessive criticism of others, and the patience to help others develop their own unique powers of thought, feelings, and actions. Given the emphasis on "individualism" in the U.S., it is not surprising that introductory psychology books give almost no space to these skills. Instead, the old psychology, like most of our educational system, supports the "myth of individualism." Competition and individualism begin from the first grades of school when they are called "cheating" and they extend throughout a person's academic career, including the Ph.D. process which must be done without assistance, and the tenure process. In psychology departments, co-authored papers are often discounted as evidence for tenure because they do not prove the "individual competence" of the candidate. It is a myth that the U.S. is ruled by such "individualism." In fact, the bankers, corporation managers, military officers, and government officials derive their power not from individualism but from a network of collective action and affiliation. It is even indicated in the words they use such as "corporations."

What are the factors that cause people to affiliate? What are the qualities that an organization needs in order to involve more people in its work? What is the psychology of recruiting and training new members? How does one design an organization and train its members so that it can analyze situations clearly and take effective action? These are some of the questions that the new psychology will face. Here we may take advantage of the work previously done by industrial and management psychology that was developed to serve capitalist business. In order to answer these questions, the new psychologists will have to be themselves affiliated so that they speak from practical experience. Already, we have such groups as Psychologists for Social Responsibility, as well as similar groups for Educators and Physicians and the more traditional peace and justice organizations, where psychologists can develop and practice the skills of affiliation.

The new psychology has a special role to play in helping activists achieve personal integration of their political lives. Burnout becomes more of a risk when activists are faced with an increasing number of potential actions and organizational commitments. If one tries to engage in every action and work with every organization, the task becomes overwhelming. Instead, activists must learn to share the load with others and develop a stable and supportive family and work situation for sustainable, long-term activity.

It is true that the clinical practice of psychotherapy is devoted to the issues of personal integration, but by itself that is not enough. Without the explicit commitment to values of peace and justice, and to action in the cause of these values, the practice of psychotherapy leads only to individualism, the satisfaction of private needs, and withdrawal from the struggles of history which is the only arena in which consciousness can fully develop. We need to develop more "movement psychotherapists" who place the problems of personal integration squarely within the framework of commitment to action and affiliation for peace and justice. Rather than practicing in isolated fashion or small groups, as is done today, the new clinicians should be joined together as a major component of the new psychology and the peace movement as a whole.

Finally, the highest challenge to the new psychology is to help train leaders of the peace movement who have attained world-historic consciousness. As developed by Debs, DuBois, and King, such leadership overcomes sectarianism and unifies all anti-war constituencies into one great working force for peace. It knows the mood of the people. It can analyze the strengths and weaknesses of all political forces in a systemic and radical, not superficial, way. It organizes and broadens the political character of the movement to keep it in step with history. And today, unlike any time in the past, it must grasp and express the emerging vision of peace and give inspiration to the peace movement for the decisive struggles ahead.

The task of developing leadership with world-historic consciousness is not a task for psychology alone, but is a central task of the peace movement as a whole, in which the new psychology should be thoroughly integrated. Out of the peace movement there will emerge leaders who have the qualities of world-historic consciousness and who have made their work for peace not only a profession, but the very core of their being. As Debs puts it, these are the "social builders." Helping to recognize and develop such leaders is the highest task to which the new psychology is called.

FOOTNOTES

1.   The Freedom Charter of the African National Congress became the vision that inspired their overthrown of the apartheid system and establishment of a peaceful democracy in South Africa. The Charter's demands of democracy, human rights and an economy of peace are essential for a culture of peace, and they can serve as a vision for peace activists throughout the world. Most of its provisions are universal in character and many are not yet fulfilled even in the richest countries.

FREEDOM CHARTER

PREAMBLE

We, the people of South Africa, declare for all our country and the world to know:

That South Africa belongs to all who live in it, black and white, and that no government can justly claim authority unless it is based on the will of the people.

That our people have been robbed of their birthright to land, liberty and peace by a form of government founded on injustice and inequality;

That our country will never been prosperous or free until all our people live in brotherhood, enjoying equal rights and opportunities;

That only a democratic state, based on the will of all the

people, can secure to all their birthright without distinction of colour, race, sex or belief;

And therefore, we the people of South Africa, black and white, together-equals, countrymen and brothers - adopt this Freedom Charter. And we pledge ourselves to strive together, sparing nothing of our strength and courage, until the democratic changes here set out have been won.

THE PEOPLE SHALL GOVERN!

Every man and woman shall have the right to vote for and stand as a candidate for all bodies which make laws;

All the people shall be entitled to take part in the administration of the country;

The rights of the people shall be the same regardless of race, colour, or sex;

All bodies of minority rule, advisory boards, councils and authorities shall be replaced by democratic organs of self-government.

ALL NATIONAL GROUPS SHALL HAVE EQUAL RIGHTS!

There shall be equal status in the bodies of state, in the courts, and in the schools, for all national groups and races;

All people shall have equal rights to use their own language and to develop their own folk cultures and customs;

All national groups shall be protected by law against insults to their race and national pride;

The preaching and practice of national, race or colour discrimination and contempt shall be a punishable crime;

All apartheid laws and practices shall be set aside.

THE PEOPLE SHALL SHARE IN THE COUNTRY'S WEALTH

The national wealth of our country, the heritage of all South Africans, shall be restored to the people;

The mineral wealth beneath the soil, the banks and monopoly industry shall be transferred to the ownership of the people as a whole;

All other industries and trade shall be controlled to assist the well-being of the people;

All people shall have equal rights to trade where they choose, to manufacture and to enter all trades, crafts and professions.

THE LAND SHALL BE SHARED AMONG THOSE WHO

WORK IT!

Restrictions of land ownership on a racial basis shall be ended, and all the land re-divided amongst those who work for it, to banish famine and land hunger.

The state shall help the peasants with implements, see, tractors and dams to save the soil and assist the tiller;

Freedom of movement shall be guaranteed to all who work on the land;

All shall have the right to occupy land wherever they choose;

People shall not be robbed of their cattle, and forced labour and farm prisons shall be abolished.

ALL SHALL BE EQUAL BEFORE THE LAW!

No one shall be imprisoned, deported or restricted without a fair trial;

No one shall be condemned by the order of any government official;

The courts shall be representatives of all the people;

Imprisonment shall be only for serious crime against the

people, and shall aim at re-education; not vengeance;

All laws which discriminate on grounds of race, colour or belief shall be repealed.

ALL SHALL ENJOY EQUAL HUMAN RIGHTS!

The law shall guarantee to all their right to speak, to organize, to meet together, to publish, to preach, to worship and to educate their children;

The privacy of the house from policy raids shall be protected by the law;

All shall be free to travel without restriction from countryside to town, from province to province, and from South Africa abroad;

Pass laws, permits and all others laws restricting these freedoms shall be abolished.

THERE SHALL BE WORK AND SECURITY!

All who work shall be free to form trade unions, to elect their officers and to make wage agreements with their employers;

The state shall recognize the right and duty of all to work and to draw full unemployment benefits;

Men and women of all races shall receive equal pay for equal work;

There shall be a forty-hour working week, a national minimum wage, paid annual leave, and sick leave for all workers, and maternity leave on full pay for all working mothers;

Miners, domestic workers, farm workers and civil servants shall have the same rights as all others who work;

Child labour, compound labour, the tot system and contract labour shall be abolished.

THE DOORS OF LEARNING AND OF CULTURE SHALL BE OPENED!

The government shall discover, develop and encourage national talent for the enhancement of our cultural life;

All the cultural treasures of mankind shall be open to all, by free exchange of books, ideas and contact with other lands;

The aim of education shall be to teach the youth to love their people and their culture, to honour human brotherhood, liberty and peace;

Education shall be free, compulsory, universal and equal for all children;

Higher education and technical training shall be opened to all by means of state allowances and scholarships awarded on the basis of merit;

Adult illiteracy shall be ended by a mass state education plan;

Teachers shall have all the rights of other citizens;

The colour bar in cultural life, in sport and in education shall be abolished.

THERE SHALL BE HOUSES, SECURITY AND COMFORT!

All people shall have the right to live where they choose, to be decently housed, and to bring up their families in comfort and security;

Unused housing space to be made available to the people;

Rent and princes shall be lowered, food plentiful and no one shall go hungry;

A preventive health scheme shall be run by the state;

Free medical care and hospitalization shall be provided for all, with special care for mothers and young children;

Slums shall be demolished, and new suburbs built where all have transport, roads, lighting, playing fields, crèches and social centres;

The aged, the orphans, the disabled and the sick shall be cared for by the state;

Rest, leisure and recreation shall be the right of all;

Fenced locations and ghettos shall be abolished, and laws which break up families shall be repealed.

THERE SHALL BE PEACE AND FRIENDSHIP!

South Africa shall be a full independent state which respects the rights and sovereignty of all nations;

South Africa shall strive to maintain world peace and the settlement of all international disputes by negotiation - not war;

Peace and friendship amongst all our people shall be secured by upholding the equal rights, opportunities and status of all;

The people of the protectorates - Basutoland, Bechuanaland and Swaziland -shall be free to decide for themselves their own future;

The right of all the people of Africa to independence and self-government shall be recognized, and shall be the basis of close co-operation.

Let all who love their people and their country now say, as we say here:

"THESE FREEDOMS WE WILL FIGHT FOR, SIDE BY SIDE, THROUGHOUT OUR LIVES, UNTIL WE HAVE WON OUR LIBERTY."

2.   The analysis of steps of consciousness development is drawn rather loosely from Soviet activity psychology as found in Methodological and Theoretical Problems of Psychology, by Boris F. Lomov, Science Publishers, Moscow, 1984. A rather similar analysis is implicit in the study by Jerome Frank and Earl Nash (Commitment to Peace Work, **American Journal of Orthopsychiatry** 35, 106-119, 1965) in which they interviewed anti-war activists and asked them how they had come to be active.   In particular, Frank and Nash called attention to the importance of anger, action, and affiliation.   There is also a strong similarity between the approach used here and that described by Paulo Friere in his well known book, **Pedagogy of the Oppressed** (Continuum Publishing, New York, 1970).

3.   The present book is based upon my study of the U.S. peace movements, copyright in 1985 and entitled: **The American Peace Movements: History, Root Causes, and Future.** I undertook that study because I am convinced that psychology must be rooted deeply in the historical context, and our historical context is concerned with war and peace. At the same time as that book was written, a more traditional history, totally ignoring the role of the Left in the peace movements of the 1930's and early Cold War, was published under the title:

The American Peace Movement: History and Historiography, by Charles Howlett and Glen Zeitzer, American Historical Association Pamphlet 261.

4. Not only is there a logical sequence to these six steps of conscious-ness, but we also find them described in rough chronological order in the autobiographies and biographies of the great peace activists. This is demonstrated by the following table that lists the page numbers in the source books for the quotations that are cited in this book. Asterisks indicate quotations that would not be expected to occur in chronological order because they are later retrospections about the step of consciousness involved.

Addams: **Book I - Twenty Years at Hull House,** Macmillan, 1910.
Book II - The Second Twenty Years at Hull House, Macmillan, 1930.
Peace and Break in Time of War, Macmillan, 1922.

Balch: **Improper Bostonian: Emily Greene Balch,** by Mercedes M. Randall,   Dwayne Publishers (New York), 1964.

Caldicott: **Nuclear Madness; What You Can Do!** Bantam Books, 1978.

Day: **The Long Loneliness**, Harper & Bros., 1952.

Debs: **The Bending Cross: A Biography of Eugene Victor Debs,** by Ray   Ginger, Rutgers University Press, 1949.

DuBois: **The Autobiography of W.E.B. DuBois,** International Publishers,   1968.

King: **Stride Toward Freedom: The Montgomery Stor**y, Harper & Bros.,   1958.
My Life with Martin Luther King, Jr., by Coretta Scott King,   Holt, Rinehart and Winston, 1969.

Mandela: **Long Walk to Freedom: The Autobiography of Nelson Mandela,** Little   Brown and Company, 1994.

Muste: **The Essays of A.J. Muste** (Sketches for an Autobiography), edited   by Nat Hentoff, Simon and Schuster, 1967.

Pollack: **Sandy Pollack: Her Life.** U. S. Peace Council, 1985.

Russell: **The Autobiography of Bertrand Russell,** republished by Simon &   Schuster.
Volume I, 1961, Allen and Unwin.
Volume II, 1968, Allen and Unwin.
Volume III, 1969, Allen and Unwin.

SOURCE	ACQUISITION	ANGER	ACTION	AFFILIATION	INTEGRATION	WORLD HISTORIC
Addams	63,76-77 115*,121*	68	85	151	Peace and Bread p.139	II-7 II-380-381
Balch	48	124	133	157,283	396	345,346
Caldicott		4,4	4,5	90*		70
Day	38,78 138	77,121*	50-51	229*	157,171	Preface*
Debs (Ginger)	21			450*	205,347	
Debs (Writings)	44	8	43,45-47	424		44,45 427,433
DuBois	112,170*	222,248	208*,248	253	279-282	269,297 400
M. King	19,131* 104-106*	39,42 102*121* 132-133* 136-137*	21 35-36			
C. King	97,224*			163	300	292,312,4*
Muste	5,46		51-52	57,84-86		149
Pollack	8		9,11	17,21		11,26
Russell	I-185	II-6 II-21,41	II-17	II-35		III-186 III-328

In addition to the sources listed above, a few quotations in the text are derived from additional sources. Quotations from A.J. Muste on pages 25, 41 and 53 are from **Abraham Went Out: A Biography of A.J. Muste,** by Jo Ann Robinson, Temple University Press, 1981, pages 21, 25, and 141 respectively, and the long quotation from Muste on page 53 is from **Peace Agitator, the Story of A.J. Muste**, by Nat Hentoff, Macmillan, 1963, page 16. The quotes on pages 16 and 22 from Helen Caldicott are from an interview with here published in the **New Haven Advocat**e May 5, 1986. The quotes on pages 25, 48, and 50 from Martin Luther King Jr. are taken from his tribute to

W.E.G. DuBois printed in **Freedomway**s, 1968, Second Quarter, pages 104-111. The quotations from biographies of Bertrand Russell and Jane Addams on pages 36 and 43 are from **The Life of Bertrand Russell** by Ronald Clark, London, 1975 (page 603), and **The Life and Legend of Jane Addam**s, by Allen Davis, New York, 1973 (footnote 435 on page 306).

5.   In a scientific paper, The Role of Anger in the Consciousness Development of Peace Activists: Where Physiology and History Intersect (International Journal of Psychophysiology, 1986, 4: 157-164) I argue that "anger is the personal fuel in the social motor that resolves the institutional contradictions that arise in the course of history." In addition to autobiographical citiations such as those in the present book, I examine the evolution of anger, beginning with anger that is triggered by attributes of the opponent (in rodents), to anter that is triggered by actions of the opponent (in primates), to anger that is triggered by injustice (in humans).   Drawing on the work of J.R. Averill **(Anger and Aggression: An Essay on Emotion,** Springer, 1984), I conclude that most human anger is anger at perceived injustice, and that anger, rather than being a negative emotion, is one that often leades to positive resultsin interpersonal relations and in the processes of history.

6.   My own experience with police-sponsored terrorism came during the Vietnam War when I was working as a journalist with the community newspaper **Modern Times** in New Haven. A series of terrorist bombings during the fall of 1969 against the headuarters of multi-national corporations culminated just before the largest of the national peace

demonstrations in November. Mass media headlined the bombings and used them to dissuade people from going to the Washington cemonstration because of the "danger of violence". The small group who did the bombings were then arrested after the demonstration and put on trial. Somer were members of the "underground" newspaper called, appropriately, "The Rat." But the person who supplied the dynamite and the expertise never came to trial because he was a government agent. A similar event had happened the year before in New Haven where one of the leaders of the anti-war protest, a Black militant who was one of the "Seven Angry Men" was arrested for a plot to dynamite various public buildings. Once again the dynamite was supplied by someone working for the government. In those days, we came to assume that anyone who spoke about dynamite was a government agent.

7.   For readers who are interested in brain physiology, the evidence for the direct neural inhibition of anger by fear is contained in the following publications: Motivational Systems of Agonistic Behavior in Muroid Rodents: A Comparative Review and Neural Model, **Aggressive Behavior**, 6: 295-346, 1980 (see pages 328-329); J.W. Mink and D.B. Adams, Why Offense is Reduced When Rats Are Tested in a Strange Cage, **Physiology and Behavio**r, 1981, 26: 567-573; and Brain Mechanisms for Offense, Defense, and Submission, **The Behavioral and Brain Science**s, 2: 201-241, 1979.

8.   For many of the readers of preliminary versions of this book, the question of anger has been the most controversial.

One effective activist wrote to me, "There is a wealth of scientific research showing that anger is a harmful emotion. Indeed, my own observations are that peace groups tend to be much less angry than groups that oppose peace groups. True, even many peace groups slip into some anger on occasion. I think that this weakens the impact of their work and certainly does not strengthen it or given it energy....We don't need another firebombing for peace and I am afraid that that is where anger too often leads." Another person wrote that "I would focus on love and oneness rather than anger, because I believe that the great problems of injustice in society are not solved at all by the behavior of activists....activists end up becoming just like the aggressor, if you will. I have found no love in any of the peace groups in which I have been involved, and certainly no peace. All I have experienced is anger and aggression. In my view this is not transcendence, but rather a perpetuation of the stalemate." This latter comment is from a psychotherapist who has been, as indicated, both active and affiliated, but has given up on it. I think that it supports the view that anger, and the acceptance of anger, is necessary for consciousness development. For a history of the suppression of anger in U.S. history, see **Anger: The Struggle for Emotional Control in America's History**, by Carol Zisowitz Stearns and Peter Stearns, University of Chicago Press, 1986.

9.   In a study of student activism, Sarah Bosch and I found that students who believe that war is part of human nature are less likely to engage in peace activism. This seems to be a true causal relationship because the correlation holds up after other factors are removed by the statistical method of partial

correlations, including the influence of family, friends and school, belief about the efficacy of action, and level of anger. Our paper, entitled The Myth That War Is Intrinsic to Human Nature Discourages Action for Peace by Young People, has been published in the book **Essays in Violence** by Ramirez, Hinde and Groebel, University of Seville, Spain, 1987. Our results replicated preliminary findings reported from Finland by the peace researcher Riitta Wahlström. Dr. Wahlström and I were among 20 scientists who took part in drafting The Seville Statement on Violence, which states categorically that war is not intrinsic to human nature:

STATEMENT ON VIOLENCE

Believing that is our responsibility to address from our particular disciplines the most dangerous and destructive activities of our species, violence and war; recognizing that science is a human cultural product which cannot be definitive or all-encompassing; and gratefully acknowledging the support of the authorities of Seville and representatives of the Spanish UNESCO; we, the undersigned scholars from around the world and from relevant sciences, have met and arrived at the following Statement on Violence. In it, we challenge a number of alleged biological findings that have been used, even by some in our disciplines, to justify violence and war. Because the alleged findings have contributed to an atmosphere of pessimism in our time, we submit that the open, considered rejection of these mis-statements can contribute significantly to the International Year of Peace.

Misuse of scientific theories and data to justify violence and war is not new but has been made since the advent of modern science. For example, the theory of evolution has been used to justify not only war, but also genocide, colonialism, and suppression of the weak.

We state our position in the form of five propositions. We are aware that there are many other issues about violence and war that could be fruitfully addressed from the standpoint of our disciplines, but we restrict ourselves here to what we consider a most important first step.

IT IS SCIENTIFICALLY INCORRECT to say that we have inherited a tendency to make war from our animal ancestors. Although fighting occurs widely throughout animal species, only a few cases of destructive intra-species fighting between organized groups have ever been reported among naturally living species, and none of these involve the use of tools designed to be weapons. Normal predatory feeding upon other species cannot be equated with intra-species violence. Warfare is a peculiarly human phenomenon and does not occur in other animals.

The fact that warfare has changed so radically over time indicates that it is a product of culture. Its biological connection is primarily through language which makes possible the coordination of groups, the transmission of technology, and the use of tools. War is biologically possible, but it is not inevitable, as evidenced by its variation in occurrence and nature over time and space. There are cultures which have not engaged in war for centuries, and there are cultures which have engaged in war frequently at some times and not at others

IT IS SCIENTIFICALLY INCORRECT to say that war or any other violent behavior is genetically programmed into our human nature. While genes are involved at all levels of nervous system function, they provide a developmental potential that can be actualized only in conjunction with the ecological and social environment. While individuals vary in their predispositions to be affected by their experience, it is the interaction between their genetic endowment and conditions of nurturance that determines their personalities Except for rare pathologies, the genes do not produce individuals necessarily predisposed to violence.   Neither do they determine the opposite.   While genes are co-involved in establishing our behavioral capacities, they do not by themselves specify the outcome.

IT IS SCIENTIFICALLY INCORRECT to say that in the course of human evolution there has been a selection for aggressive behavior more than for other kinds of behavior. In all well-studied species, status within the group is achieved by the ability to cooperate and to fulfil social functions relevant to the structure of that group.   "Dominance" involves social bondings and affiliations; it is not simply a matter of the possession and use of superior physical power, although it does include aggressive behaviors Where genetic selection for aggressive behavior has been artificially instituted in animals, it has rapidly succeeded in producing hyper-aggressive individuals; this indicates that aggression was not maximally selected under natural conditions. When such experimentally-created hyper-aggressive animals are present in a social group, they either disrupt its social structure or are driven out. Violence is neither in our evolutionary legacy nor in our genes.

IT IS SCIENTIFICALLY INCORRECT to say that humans have a "violent brain." While we do have the neural apparatus to act violently, it is not automatically activated by internal or external stimuli Like higher primates and unlike other animals, our higher neural processes filter such stimuli before they can be acted upon. How we act is shaped by how we have been conditioned and socialized. There is nothing in our neurophysiology that compels us to react violently.

IT IS SCIENTIFICALLY INCORRECT to say that war is caused by "instinct" or any single motivation. The emergence of modern warfare has been a journey from the primacy of emotional and motivational factors, sometimes called "instincts," to the primacy of cognitive factors. Modern war involves institutional use of personal characteristics such as obedience, suggestibility, and idealism, social skills such as language, and rational considerations such as cost-calculation, planning, and information processing. The technology of modern war has exaggerated traits associated with violence both in the training of actual combatants and in the preparation of support for war in the general population. As a result of this exaggeration, such traits are often mistaken to be the causes rather than the consequences of the process.

128

We conclude that biology does not condemn humanity to war, and that humanity can be freed from the bondage of biological pessimism and empowered with confidence the undertake the transformative tasks needed in this International Year of Peace and in the years to come. Although these tasks are mainly institutional and collective, they also rest upon the consciousness of individual participants for whom pessimism and optimism are crucial factors. Just as "wars begin the minds of men," peace also begins our minds. The same species who invented war is capable of inventing peace. The responsibility lies with each of us.

Seville, May 16, 1986

David Adams, Psychology, Wesleyan University, Middletown (CT) USA.
S. A. Barnett, Ethology, The Australian National University, Canberra, Australia
N. P. Bechtereva, Neurophysiology, Institute for Experimental Medicine of Academy of Medical Sciences of USSR, Leningrad, USSR.
Bonnie Frank Carter, Psychology, Albert Einstein Medical Center, Philadelphia (PA) USA.
José M. Rodriguez Delgado, Neurophysiology, Centro de Estudios Neurobiologicos, Madrid, Spain.
José Luis Diaz, Ethology, Instituto Mexicano de Psiquiatria, Mexico D.F, Mexico.
Andrzej Eliasz, Individual Differences Psychology, Polish Academy of Sciences, Warsaw, Poland.

Santiago Genovés, Biological Anthropology, Instituto de
Estudios Antropologicos, Mexico D.F., Mexico.
Benson E. Ginsburg, Behavior Genetics, University of
Connecticut, Storrs (CT) USA.

Jo Groebel, Social Psychology, Erziehungswissenschaftliche
Hochschule,Landau, Federal Republic of Germany.
Samir-Kumar Ghosh, Sociology, Indian Institute of Human
Sciences, Calcutta, India.
Robert Hinde, Animal Behavior, Cambridge University, UK.
Richard E. Leakey, Physical Anthropology, National Museums
of Kenya, Nairobi, Kenya.
Taha H. Malasi, Psychiatry, Kuwait University, Kuwait.
J. Martin Ramirez, Psychobiology, Univeridad de Sevilla, Spain.
Federico Mayor Zaragoza, Biochemistry, Universidad
Autonoma, Madrid, Spain.
Diana L. Mendoza, Ethology, Universidad de Sevilla, Spain.
Ashis Nandy, Political Psychology, Center for the Study of
Developing Societies, Delhi, India.
John Paul Scott, Animal Behavior, Bowling Green State
University, Bowling Green (OH) USA.
Riitta Wahlstrom, Psychology, University of Jyvaskyla, Finland.

10.   Every mass peace movement in this century in the U.S.
has been attacked by anti-communism, and in many cases
actually destroyed.   When William Jennings Bryan ran for
President in 1900 on an anti-imperialist platform put forward by
the Anti-Imperialist League, he was attacked by his Vice-
Presidential opponent Theodore Roosevelt, as "communistic."
The People's Council of America, the mass opposition to World

War I was literally smashed by government agents who seized their mail, raided their offices, and imprisoned their leaders - all in the name of anti-communism. The peace movement of the 1930's opposed to the rise of fascism was split into two competing organizations, one that included Communist participation and the other that was based on anti-communism. The opposition to the Cold War that culminated in the Wallace Presidential campaign was not only destroyed by anti-communism, but is not even mentioned in today's "official" histories of the peace movement (see footnote 3). And opposition to the Vietnam War was set back by the anti-communism of the traditional peace movement organizations such as SANE who refused to take part in demonstrations alongside such organizations as SDS because they were "communist." For further details, see **The American Peace Movements** (footnote 3) and the references listed therein.

11.   With the end of the Cold War, people tend to forget certain accomplishments of the socialist countries in the development of a peace economy. They avoided the cyclical overproduction and crises of unemployment of the capitalist countries and the exploitation which characterizes the relations of the major capitalist powers to the developing world. The latter is documented by the lead article of the November 29, 1985 issue of **Science.** In this article the dean of Rand Corporation's graduate school, a Pentagon supported think-tank, shows that the net flow of wealth was from the Soviet Union to the smaller socialist countries and the Third World, a flow which was actually increasing rather than decreasing at the time This was is contrast to the US. and other Western

powers who profit greatly from their foreign economic relations The author asks what are the benefits of Soviet foreign economic relations and replies that they are "prestige, political prominence, Russian national pride, and justification for the sacrifices imposed on the Soviet populace by the Soviet system." These reasons are quite different from the basis of imperialism according to the classic definition of Hobson: the use of government machinery to secure economic gains abroad.

12. The overall effect of military production in U.S. society should be considered as a negative factor in any accounting of the economy's strength. This is explained by economist Lloyd Dumas in **The Overburdened Economy,** University of California Press, 1986. The development of peace economies would be aided by a new approach to the study of economics following along the lines proposed by Professor Dumas in this book.

13. See my article, Internal Military Interventions in the United States, **Journal of Peace Research,** Vol.31, no.2, 1995.

14. At one time it was thought that fear would be a good motivation for attitude change (e.g. for Madison Avenue advertising, heal education, etc.). However, when the relevant studies were done, it was found that fear is not an effective motivation for changing attitudes and behavior. Instead of changing their attitudes, people tend to become more resistant to change when they are made afraid. For a technical review

of the scientific studies, see Effects of Fear Arousal on Attitude Change, by Irving L. Janis, **Advances in Experimental Social Psychology,** 3: 167-224, 1967.

15. For many who work in the mass media, the decision to emphasize pessimistic rather than optimistic news is probably made without any particular awareness of its effects, and simply as a consequence of the fact that optimistic news often tends to involve criticism of advertisers (e.g. news of trade unions and community organizing) and the military-industrial complex (news from the peace movement). For others, however, the use of pessimism can be a deliberate device as part of the culture of war. In his article, CIA Psychological Warfare Operations (Science for the People, pp. 6-11 and 29-37, January/February, 1982), Fred Landis carefully documents how the CIA emphasized and fabricated pessimistic news as part of their psychological warfare when they took over the operation of newspapers in countries on the verge of revolutionary change. In particular, he documents the transformations of the newspapers El Mercurio in Chile, Daily Gleaner in Jamaica, and La Prensa in Nicaragua after they were taken over by the CIA.